Old College, Aberystwyth

Old College, Aberystwyth

The Evolution of a
High Victorian Building

J. ROGER WEBSTER

UNIVERSITY OF WALES PRESS

CARDIFF

1995

British Library Cataloguing-in-Publication Data
A catalogue record for this book is available from the British Library.

ISBN 0-7083-1286-1

The publishers wish to acknowledge the financial assistance of the Margaret and Gwendoline Davies Charities towards the cost of producing this volume.

Cover design by Design Principle, Cardiff
Typeset at the University of Wales Press
Printed in Great Britain by Henry Ling Ltd., The Dorset Press, Dorchester, Dorset

Contents

Illustrations

Preface

It is a bitter-sweet privilege to write the preface to this book. Bitter, because Roger Webster died on 30 March 1995 before he could read the proofs. Sweet, because the book *is* published, against odds which seemed at times overwhelming. I first knew of this fascinating work when he had despaired of its publication. The cost of publishing the book was inevitably increased by the cost of the photographs and plans which illuminate the text. The Davies Charities' long association with Aberystwyth made the trustees a willing donor of the sum required to guarantee this publication. As one trustee, I had the pleasant task of telling Roger Webster that the money had been secured.

This book is likely to be, in Auden's words about a poet's hope,

> like some valley cheese,
> local, but prized elsewhere.

It *is* local. Roger Webster, from 1978 until 1991, worked in the Old College at Aberystwyth as Professor of Education and Dean of Education. His eyes and mind were alert to the peculiar charm of the building where he had also been a student. His painstaking research now offers new insights on the building and on Seddon, its architect. His sensitivity, which made him an outstanding Director of the Welsh Arts Council for five years, pervades the work and enables us to appreciate Seddon's artistic achievements in architecture, one of the great creative arts of the Victorian age.

Throughout his career Roger Webster returned to the theme of education and the arts as social activities. 'The Place of Secondary Education in Welsh Society 1800–1918' was the title of his doctoral thesis. He wrote a fine book on *School and Community in Rural Wales*. This book on Old College now published will surely confirm the importance of Seddon and his building in the history of architecture, an art form which has to be involved visibly with its society. It is immensely sad that Roger Webster did not live to greet its publication.

Tom Arfon Owen

Acknowledgements

I have had help in locating material from the Maps and Prints Department of the National Library of Wales, the Victoria and Albert Museum and the British Architectural Library and Archives Department. Dr Ian Salmon guided me through the College archives. Mr Richard Brinkley of the Hugh Owen Library shared with me his wide knowledge of the history of the College and made available the illustrative material which he has gathered over the years, while Professor Alistair Crawford arranged the photographing of materials in his care. Professor K. O. Morgan kindly read an early draft and made a number of valuable comments. I have also received help on specific points from Mr Peter Hendry, Mr Dafydd Gapper, Mr Phil Thomas and Professor Bernard Dietrich. My daughter, Catrin, made the sketch of the Old College library as originally designed by Seddon. My wife has given me constant support, particularly in preparing the manuscript for the Press at a time when illness made this difficult for me.

My greatest debt is to Mr Tom Arfon Owen who shares my enthusiasm for the Old College building; without his diplomatic skills and persistence this book would not have been published. I am deeply grateful to him.

J. Roger Webster
1 March 1995

The publishers would like to thank the following for their kind permission to reproduce illustrations:

The British Architectural Library, RIBA, London
   Nos. 6, 8, 9, 10, 27, 31, 35, 45.

Michael Murray
   Nos. 17, 19, 20, 21, 22, 23, 26, 34, 38, 42, 43, 46.

National Library of Wales
   Nos. 1 (T. Lloyd Collection), 2, 3, 11, 12, 13, 14, 30, 33.

National Monuments Record of Wales (RCAHMW)
   Nos. 4, 28.

University College of Wales, Aberystwyth
   Nos. 5, 15, 16, 18, 29, 32, 37, 40, 41 (photograph by Ron Davies),
   44, and the plans of Old College on pp. 85–7.

V & A Picture Library, Victoria & Albert Museum
   Nos. 7, 24, 25

Catrin Webster
   No. 39.

1

Castle House

Old College, Aberystwyth, is a spectacular High Victorian building, but there resides within it the ghost of an earlier 'Gothic' house that partly determined its idiosyncratic ground-plan and encouraged its anarchic architecture. This was Castle House, built in the early 1790s by Uvedale Price as a holiday home for his wife, Lady Caroline. Although the architect of Castle House was John Nash, it was Price who insisted on its radical design, and thus established the aesthetic out of which Old College was ultimately to emerge.

Uvedale Price (1747–1829) was a wealthy landowner; he was fortunate to have inherited, not only the family estate at Foxley, Herefordshire, but also a considerable fortune. While a pupil at Eton, Price developed a lifelong friendship with the Whig politician Charles James Fox and, in 1767–8, they went on a Grand Tour of Europe which included a visit to Voltaire at Férény. Although Price became a Whig member of Parliament, his main interest was in agricultural improvement and in making his estate more picturesque. Thus he contributed to Arthur Young's *Annals of Agriculture* and, more significantly, in 1794 published his *Essay on the Picturesque*, which made him, in the view of one art historian, the 'most sensible, evocative and influential explicator' of the major aesthetic movement in eighteenth-century Britain.[1] In common with similarly wealthy young Englishmen who had been on the Grand Tour, the way in which Price perceived the world was transformed once he became acquainted with the works of seventeenth-century French and Italian landscape painters, such as Nicolas Poussin, Salvator Rosa, Gaspard Dughet and, pre-eminently, Claude Lorrain with his depiction of a harmonious and balanced ideal classical world. The term 'Picturesque' is derived from the Italian *pittoresco* ('after the manner of painters'), and the Picturesque movement provided a conceptual framework which enabled the English educated classes to interpret, not only the content and composition of landscape paintings, but also the natural landscape, the layout of estates and the design of buildings in relation to the landscape. Thus Price included in the title of his essay on the Picturesque the phrase *The Use of Studying Pictures, for the Purpose of Improving Real Landscape.*[2]

Initially, the object of picturesque landscaping was to replace the French and Dutch formal garden with turf and woodland, arranged irregularly and asymmetrically, to create a sequence of classically structured 'pictures'. Following Chinese practice and, more particularly, the example of the Italian landscape painters, these vistas were often embellished with evocative grottoes, temples, cascades and wildernesses and, increasingly as the century progressed, with Gothic follies and simulated ruins. Increasingly, too, Palladian mansions were replaced by houses built in a variety of Gothic designs.[3] Thus, during the second half of the century, and certainly by the 1790s when Price was writing his treatise and was building Castle House, the theory of Picturesque landscaping had taken a new direction. This had been signalled in 1757 by the young Edmund Burke when he suggested that the impact of a picture, landscape or building depended on the individual sensations that it aroused, and not on abstract mathematical rules of composition or, in the case of architecture, on a relationship with the ideal proportions of the human body. Burke, therefore, differentiated between the 'sublime', which he associated with 'terror, obscurity and the infinite', and the 'beautiful' whose attributes were 'smallness, smoothness, gradual variation and delicacy of form'.[4] Burke's aesthetic categories, which depended on an individual's subjective responses rather than on abstract classical rules, signalled the beginning of the Romantic movement. It was certainly the starting-point for Price's essay.

Within Burke's categorization, it was the aim of the best-known landscape gardener of the eighteenth century, Lancelot 'Capability' Brown, to achieve the 'beautiful'. In redesigning his clients' estates, Brown eliminated cultivated fields, farm buildings, kitchen gardens and any evidence of economic activity, or of the existence of a tenantry and workers, and then 'smoothed' nature to produce gentle lawns, serpentine streams and lakes, strategically placed clumps of trees, soft wooded hills and gravel paths. His parklands, although intended to look natural, became as artificial as the most idealized landscape painting. For his clients, he created an Arcadia which isolated them from the reality of the world outside their gates. For many, however, the impact of Brown's landscaping soon began to pall. In the 1750s and 1760s, at the time his influence was at its height, enclosures and 'improvement' were changing the face of lowland Britain. Partly as a reaction to this movement, tours to the remoter areas of the country were becoming popular, especially to the Lake District, the highlands of Scotland and to Wales – all of which were areas that provided an experience of wilder and more 'natural' landscapes; of the sublime rather than the beautiful.

One of the most influential of these tourists was the Revd William Gilpin, who, in the 1790s, defined the picturesque in a new, and more confined, way. He made a distinction between landscape features that were 'beautiful' and 'sublime', as defined by Burke, and those that were 'picturesque', which, although comparatively small in scale and in no way awesome, were characterized by roughness, irregularity and variousness and, in consequence, held greater potential as subjects for the artist than softer 'beautiful' landscapes.[5]

This was also the way in which Price defined the picturesque, although he gave the 'beautiful', the 'sublime' and the 'picturesque' equal value. As a young man, he had been fortunate to have been befriended by Thomas Gainsborough, who visited Foxley during the 1760s and allowed Price to accompany him on sketching excursions. Gainsborough's rustic landscapes, his 'fancy pictures' of ragged children and his cottage scenes, although denigrated as 'humble art' by Sir Joshua Reynolds, were precursors of the picturesque as defined by Gilpin. Price, under Gainsborough's influence, also became attracted to irregular, overgrown landscapes embellished with rustic cottages and populated by peasants, gypsies and beggars.[6] Thus, in his writings, he constantly attacks Brown's parklands as artificial because their 'open, licentious display of beauties' had replaced 'modest nature'. He was most appalled by a proposal of one of Brown's followers, William Emes, that the hanging terraces at Powis Castle be blown up, and the escarpment smoothed into a green slope!

Such landscape designers, in Price's view, ignored two of the most potent sources of human pleasure: variety and intricacy. It was his contention 'that the two opposite qualities of roughness, and of sudden variation, joined to that of irregularity' were the 'most efficient causes of the picturesque'. This was also true of architecture. Buildings had to be seen in the context of the landscape of which they were a part. The architect should 'accommodate his building to the scenery, not make [the scenery] give way to the building' – thus, the attraction of cottages as an embellishment to a rustic scene. For the same reason, Gothic architecture was 'more picturesque, though less beautiful than Grecian; and upon the same principle that a ruin is more so than a new edifice'.

The first thing that strikes the eye in approaching any building, is the general outline, the effect of the openings: in Grecian buildings, the general lines of the roof are straight, and even when varied and adorned by a dome or a pediment, the whole has a character of symmetry and regularity. But symmetry, which, in works of art particularly, accords with the beautiful, is in the same degree adverse to the picturesque; and among the various causes of the superior picturesqueness of ruins compared with entire buildings, the destruction of symmetry is by no means the least powerful.

Architects were, however, subject to a number of constraints. Although in nature straight lines were rare, the reverse was true of architecture, and 'any attempt to avoid them, must in general appear unnatural or affected'. Curves must also be 'regular and uniform', and 'angles, which certainly are not beautiful when separately considered, must perpetually occur'. Price's concern was the siting and design of buildings on estates in lowland areas. Such estates were rarely, if ever, found in sublime landscapes. In any case, it was Price's view that 'to create the sublime is above our contracted powers, though we may sometimes heighten, and at all times lower its effects by art'. But, as travel to the remoter parts of Britain became more popular, so more note had to be taken of the sublime which evoked stronger individual reactions and thus had more obvious romantic connotations.

Price was brought face to face with this issue as a result of his friendship with Thomas Johnes of Hafod. As young men, Price, Johnes and Johnes's cousin, Richard Payne Knight, all lived on neighbouring estates in Herefordshire. All three became lifelong friends, sharing the same aesthetic interests. One of the first acts of Payne Knight, when he came of age in 1771, was to rebuild Downton Castle as a castellated asymmetrical Gothic mansion, directly influenced by the paintings of Claude. Meanwhile, Price was improving his estate at Foxley by creating new vistas and laying a drive, a mile and a half long, through the woods. Thomas Johnes's roots were in Cardiganshire; but his father, on his marriage to Elizabeth Knight of Croft Castle, had moved from his modest mansion at Llanfair Clydogau to live in his wife's Herefordshire home. As Croft Castle was Gothicized during the young Thomas Johnes's childhood, he grew up in the world of the new aesthetic. On the death of his father in 1780, and then of his first wife two years later, Thomas Johnes began to take an interest in his Cardiganshire properties, and this led to his discovery of Hafod situated in a remote valley some fifteen miles inland from Aberystwyth. With the advice and encouragement of Knight and Price, he decided to create at Hafod a Welsh 'Eden'.[7] He built a new and impressive Gothic house designed by Thomas Baldwin of Bath. As to the landscaping of the estate, although Johnes added a number of picturesque features such as an alpine bridge, a Druid temple and, for his daughter Mariamne, a miniature Garden of Eden, there was no need to make extensive alterations to the valley's natural state. Johnes concentrated on planting extensive woodlands and laying out well-kept picturesque walks leading to natural features such as the waterfalls that already existed on the estate. The wildness of the landscape was thus retained. As Leslie Parris has suggested, 'at Hafod the visitor was as likely to be reminded of Salvator and Milton as of Claude and Virgil'.[8]

4

In 1794, Richard Payne Knight published his long didactic poem *The Landscape*, which was addressed to Uvedale Price and which, indeed, reiterated most of Price's ideas. Knight, too, abhorred

> Prim gravel walks, through which we winding go,
> In endless serpentines that nothing show.

'O! waft me hence', he implored, 'to some neglected vale.' Such a vale was provided at Hafod, and it was here in the 1780s that Price and Knight developed their views of the picturesque. They were attracted as much to the surrounding countryside as to the estate itself. Although the hills of Cardiganshire did not suggest the 'terror' of Snowdonia, it was difficult, for example, when standing in Mariamne's garden high above the house and looking down to the valley of the Ystwyth and the hills beyond, not to have a sense of the sublime. There was also the 'sublime of intricacy' displayed by the nearby Devil's Bridge with its cascades, depths and chasms which, in Price's view, provided 'one of the most surprisingly romantic scenes in all the principality'.[9] Creating the sublime might be 'above our contracted powers' but, amongst the hills of mid Wales, an estate such as Hafod took on an entirely different character from those designed by Capability Brown in the Home Counties. The pre-eminence of Wales, as many artists such as Turner and John Sell Cotman were to discover, was thus not its picturesqueness, but its potential to invoke romantic responses. Price's relationship to the Romantic movement of the late eighteenth and early nineteenth centuries is ambiguous. His concern was 'improvement' and, as Sir Nikolaus Pevsner has suggested, 'to improve landscape is unromantic *per se*'.

> The romantic attitude is one of exploration and self-abandon. Nature is accepted as supreme; one can spend a lifetime studying her smallest or her immeasurably greatest works; we can approach her with burning love or awe – but we can never improve her. That is the faith behind Wordsworth and Constable, behind Turner and Girtin and Cotman and the great romantic scientists of the Davy calibre.

It was also the faith that was to inspire Seddon when building Old College; but it was a faith into which Price and his friends were just beginning to be initiated.

> Knight and Price, no doubt, had more respect for nature, especially because they commanded a wider range of visual receptivity. They also – Price more than Knight – developed and analysed several of the romantic criteria of aesthetics (contrast, surprise, variety). But the very fact that they still used them to correct nature is of the Age of Reason. We can trust Shelley's instinct in such matters; and Shelley wrote to Peacock that Knight and Price 'could not catch the hare'.[10]

Whatever the truth about the extent of Price's romantic responses, it was undoubtedly in the Cardiganshire countryside that they were given their greatest encouragement. Johnes and his guests made frequent visits to Aberystwyth which, in the late eighteenth century, was developing as a fashionable watering-place. Here Price and his wife, Lady Caroline, standing on the shore under the ruins of the medieval castle, found themselves 'always on the spot, always looking at the waves breaking against the near rocks, and at the long chain of distant mountains with the monarch Snowdon at their head'.[11] So they thought 'how charming it would be [to] look at it comfortably from our window in all weathers instead of being driven away "when the strong winds do blow" just when the waves are the most magnificent.' Thus, they planned to build a summer house on that spot, and indulge their romantic instincts from the comfort of their armchairs!

The growth of Aberystwyth outside its medieval boundaries was, however, hindered by the Court Leet's reluctance to allow the town's commons to be built on. But Uvedale Price, through the influence of Thomas Johnes, was appointed a burgess, and, in 1788, was given permission to enclose a section of the foreshore, 132 yards in length, to build a summer house for his wife, provided that it was constructed in two years, that a garden was created and a road laid out on the south side.[12] Initially, Price, true to his picturesque instincts, thought 'of running up two or three nutshells of rooms' and 'got a plan from a common welch carpenter'. But then John Nash became involved. After the bankruptcy of his London practice, Nash had, in 1784, retreated to Carmarthen where, amongst other commissions, he was given work by the local gentry, beginning in 1787 with a design for a cold-water bath for the local member of Parliament, John Vaughan of Golden Grove. This led to an introduction to Thomas Johnes and to many visits to Hafod where he joined in discussions of Picturesque theory and the way in which it could be be put into practice.[13] Nash was almost certainly commissioned in 1793 to add a great octagonal Gothic library to Hafod and make a number of other alterations to the house. Earlier, Price had invited him to design his Aberystwyth summer house. Nash immediately planned a much larger house, but, as at that time he had no practical experience of Gothic, this was to be 'a square bit of architecture'. But Price had other ideas. As he later noted in a letter to Sir George Beaumont:

> I told him however that I must have, not only some of the *windows*, but some of the *rooms* turned to particular points, and that he must arrange it in his best manner: I explained to him the reasons why I built it so close to the rock, shewed him the effect of the broken foreground and its varied line, and how by that means the foreground was connected with the rocks in the second ground; all of which would be lost by placing the house further back.

6

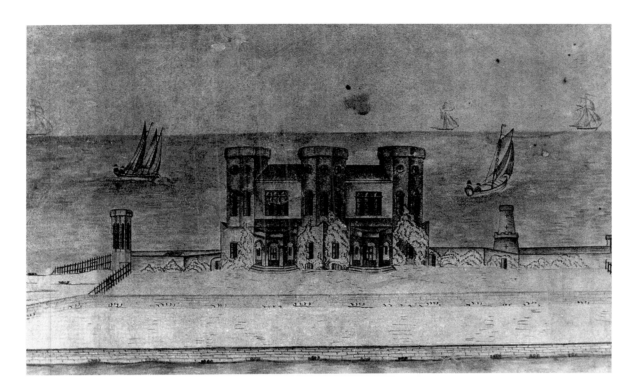

1. Engraving of Castle House, Aberystwyth, designed by John Nash in about 1794, after J. P. Neale.

Nash was patently impressed by this application of basic Claudian picture construction to appreciating landscape:

> He was excessively struck with these reasons which he said he had never thought of before in the most distant degree, and he has I think contrived the house most admirably for the situation, and the form of it is certainly extremely varied from my having obliged him to turn the rooms to different aspects. At first, as I told you, I meant only to have nutshells, but now I thought that I would have one good room; and so I magnificently ordered one of 30 by 20; a charming room it is . . .

Because of real or imaginary financial pressures 'in these pinching times', Price delayed building the house 'for at least two years'. It was, therefore, probably completed during 1791–2. It certainly must have been built earlier than *c.* 1795, as suggested by Mansbridge.[14] The dating is of significance, because the earlier date would confirm Uvedale Price's contention that Castle House was Nash's first experience of designing a picturesque building.

The original plans of Castle House are lost, but an accurate impression of the first and second floors can be obtained from plans and elevations made by Edward H. Martineau, when he made additions to the house in 1858. Seddon used these plans when he added his extensions in 1864, and, as his design for the Castle House Hotel shows,

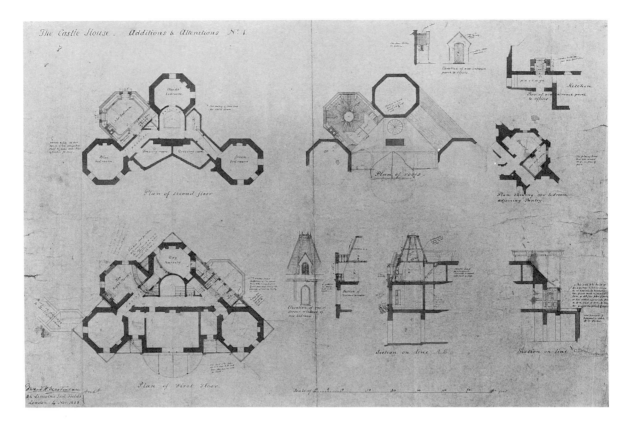

he retained Nash's ground-plan (see p.37). Nash's house was triangular in plan, with a tower at each of the angles. The ground-floor rooms in the towers, although at an angle to catch the best view, had right-angled corners. On the upper two floors, the towers turned into irregular hexagons, so that the right-angled corners of the ground-floor rooms became triangular projections (see the elevations of the rear of the house on p.9). The north tower had views of Constitution Hill and, on a clear day, of the Llŷn peninsula and the mountains of mid and north Wales (but hardly as far as 'the monarch Snowdon', as Uvedale Price suggested to Sir George Beaumont). The south tower had a view of the ruined medieval castle and the cliffs. The central room on the ground floor, called a 'saloon' by Mansbridge, had extensive views from its rounded bay, and had direct access to the terrace. This must have been the room that Price had 'magnificently ordered'. The master bedroom with a dressing room attached, on the first floor, opened to a spectacular canopied verandah above the bay of the saloon below. Following the practice instituted by the Adam brothers, and developed by Nash, the house was stuccoed.

The design of Castle House was primarily functional: to enable the

2. Plans and elevations of Nash's Castle House, drawn by Edward H. Martineau in the 1850s at the time when enlargements and additions were being planned.

8

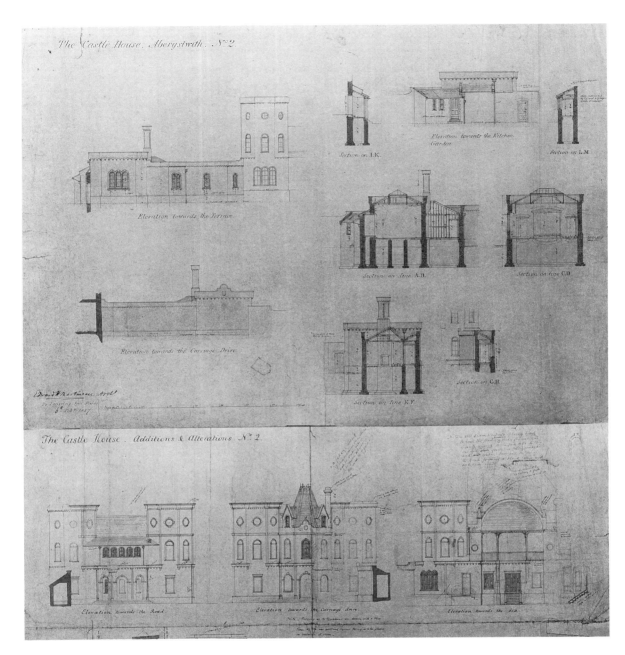

The Castle House. Abergstwith. Nº 2.

Elevation towards the Terrace

Section on I K.

Elevation towards the Kitchen Garden

Section on L M

Section on line A B.

Section on line C D.

Elevation towards the Carriage Drive

Section on line E F.

Section on G H.

The Castle House. Additions & Alterations Nº 2.

Elevation towards the Road

Elevation towards the Carriage Drive

Elevation towards the Sea

3. Martineau's elevations of Nash's Castle House, drawn in the 1850s, showing alterations.

occupants to have varied and extensive views of the Cardigan coast; it was an eighteenth-century 'machine for living in'. But it was also a picturesque building – an eye-catcher designed to embellish the landscape. Nash had achieved the main characteristics of the picturesque – asymmetry, variety and intricacy – in both plan and elevations. The house combined a range of geometrical forms. Its plan

9

was triangular, the base of the towers circular and their first and second floors hexagonal. Variety was also achieved in the fenestration, which varied from square-headed windows in the saloon to the small circular windows in the towers on the second floor. Nash's design evolved as a result of discussions with Price, but was also patently influenced by Payne Knight's Downton Castle. As his first excursion into the picturesque, Castle House was significant to the development of Nash as an architect: asymmetry was soon to become a hallmark, and some of the houses he built in the 1790s showed the direct influence of Castle House.[15]

Price's intention to create 'nutshells' was the whim of a wealthy squire, when on holiday, playing at going native, not only observing the picturesque, but pretending to be part of it. The Castle House that was ultimately built signified something different. Price had come to Aberystwyth for the scenery, not to fraternize with the locals and tourists. He was a snob, and part of his objection to the landscaping of Capability Brown was because it appealed to the *nouveau riche*; true picturesque taste could only be developed by a sensitive élite with a 'cultivated eye'.[16] It is little wonder therefore that, when he visited Aberystwyth, Price was unpopular with the locals, with a reputation for being critical of others.[17] Athough Castle House was a picturesque fancy, it also created an enclosed world with private access to the shore. Symbolically, the boundary wall was marked by two towers with lancet windows. Although the towers in the house did not have battlements, some of the windows also suggested lancets. That there were towers at all inevitably signified a fortress, even though the house had a canopied verandah and was stuccoed.

But Castle House was juxtaposed to the ruin of a genuine medieval castle, whose grounds had been laid out by Price in a series of picturesque walks. Its incongruity was, therefore, bound to strike the observer. For example, in 1816, when a Revd Mr Evans compared the 'dilapidated fragments' of the nearby 'time worn' medieval castle with Castle House, he 'could not suppress a smile, and [the] thought [that] if the heroes of antiquity could return, with what contempt they would survey this mimickry of the antique'. *The Aberystwyth Guide* which published these comments, however, defended the originality of the building. 'Would men, whether idiots or philosophers,' it suggested, 'act for themselves, the world would not be surfeited with that sameness of manner and appearance by which all ranks are too frequently governed.'[18]

It is, perhaps, not surprising that Price and his wife soon tired of Castle House. To sit in isolation observing the waves must have quickly palled. Price's glowing description of the house and its site to Sir George

10

Beaumont in 1796 was in the hope that Sir George might be persuaded to buy it. In time, too, as Aberystwyth grew as the 'Brighton of Wales', Castle House no longer stood alone. In 1807, two substantial double-fronted houses, Mount Pleasant, were built at the arched entrance to the grounds, and, in 1810, the land behind the house was leased to enable Assembly Rooms to be built, and a shrubbery and pleasure grounds created in the space between the Rooms and the house. In the event, the Assembly Rooms were not built for a further decade, although, in the mean time, the Georgian houses that became Laura Place were completed. The Assembly Rooms were designed by George Stanley Repton, the fourth son of Humphrey Repton, the landscape designer who had partnered John Nash in so many of his projects. G. S. Repton had been one of Nash's pupils and, having worked for his father for a time, set up his own practice in 1820. The Assembly Rooms were one of the first buildings that he designed independently.[19] He created a simple classical building, appropriate to the needs of Aberystwyth's polite classes who wished to emulate the social round of Bath or Regency London. Castle House and the Assembly Rooms thus faced each other, across Laura Gardens, like protagonists in a battle of styles.

It was not until 1824, two years before Lady Caroline died, that Castle House was at last sold. It became a 'superior lodging house' and later, in 1848, it was let as furnished apartments.[20] In the 1850s, however, it reverted to a private dwelling and, in 1858, Edward H. Martineau was commissioned to enlarge it. He added bedrooms to the

4. Photograph of Castle House, c. 1860.

11

first and second floors over the three-sided entrance hall. The second-floor bedroom had a new dormer window and was roofed with a spirelet. This can be seen in the photograph of the house taken in the early 1860s. At this time Castle House was again for sale. In 1864, the railway line from Machynlleth reached Aberystwyth, with connections to the Midlands and London, bringing with it the hope of a boom in the tourist industry. Plans were made to convert Castle House into a hotel. The architect employed for its conversion was John Pollard Seddon, who had a London practice but who, for ten years, from 1851 to 1862, had been a partner of John Prichard, architect to the diocese of Llandaff. Although Seddon could not have foreseen it at the time, he was to be involved with the astonishing edifice that grew around the nucleus of Castle House for the next quarter of a century. To comprehend the building that ultimately emerged, it is thus necessary to understand Seddon's architectural ideas, as they developed in the mid-Victorian period.

2

J. P. Seddon and the Gothic Revival

5. John Pollard Seddon (1827–1906). Portrait in oils by Hans Olaf Heyerdal.

When John Pollard Seddon became, in 1847, a pupil of T. L. Donaldson, professor of architecture at University College, London, the battle of styles was at its height. Donaldson was a leading neo-classicist and one of the movement's major apologists. However, the twenty-year-old Seddon had little in common with his teacher; from the beginning of his career, he was drawn into a circle of young architects who were dedicated Goths. J. P. Seddon came from a family of London cabinet-makers. The firm of Seddon, established at Aldersgate in the mid-eighteenth century, had, by the 1800s, become very successful, designing furniture for both Buckingham Palace and Windsor Castle. Inevitably, his father hoped that John, and his elder brother Thomas, would join the family firm. But, although both brothers became skilled furniture designers, their ambitions lay elsewhere: Thomas was intent on becoming a painter, John an architect.[1] Thomas was six years older than John. Throughout the 1840s he trained, in his spare time, as an artist, and even set up a 'school' in his father's premises in Gray's Inn Road that provided facilities for life studies and acted as a meeting-place for young artists. He also became a friend of Ford Madox Brown and, in turn, of Brown's pupil D. G. Rossetti. When Rossetti and his friends formed the Pre-Raphaelite Brotherhood in 1848, they found the premises in the Gray's Inn Road useful for life studies and social gatherings. At this time, John lived with Thomas and he took part in the Brotherhood's social activities. The members were all creative and lively young men in their early twenties. Even towards the end of his life, Seddon remembered vividly the meetings they had 'wherein much animated discussion took place upon artistic subjects', although he 'wished sometimes earlier closing hours than they were accustomed to, for Rossetti was apt to break them up about 3 a.m. as a rule, with a yawn, and remark that he must really go home and work'.[2]

There were other social occasions which Seddon recalled; in particular, the time when Holman Hunt invited friends to his rooms in Chelsea, 'to see the glorious background he had painted for his picture of *The Light of the World* . . . This was remarkable as being a moon-lit woodland scene, actually painted in moon-light from an extemporized studio in the open.'[3] Seddon also gained a high opinion of the work of Rossetti (the group's 'adored Gabriel') because of its 'bold and rich colouring', and he gave him a commission to paint a water-colour drawing of Giotto painting a portrait of Dante. He also bought two important oil paintings by Ford Madox Brown: *King Lear* (now in the Tate Gallery) and *An English Afternoon, Hampstead* (now in the Birmingham Museum and Art Gallery).[4] Both pictures were later bought back by the artist. Seddon's interest in art was not confined to collecting. In 1848, he accompanied his brother on an excursion to Betws-y-Coed where, together, they painted landscapes seriously for the first time.[5] Seddon himself became a competent water-colourist, as the examples of his work in the Seddon Room in Old College show. Thus, Seddon's involvement with the Pre-Raphaelites reinforced his youthful romanticism. It engendered in him an enthusiasm for pre-sixteenth-century art and architecture that was only matched by his intense dislike of the art and architecture of the High Renaissance itself. It gave him, too, his taste for bold colours and, most significant of all, his passion for 'nature'.

The main movers of the Victorian Gothic revival in architecture were A. W. N. Pugin and the writers and architects associated with the Ecclesiological Society. There was a new edition of Uvedale Price's essays on the picturesque in 1842, and they were still widely read. The Gothic architecture the Ecclesiologists espoused, however, was very different from its picturesque precursor. It was derived from an antiquarian interest in medieval buildings, which were seen as products of an age of faith and social harmony. To Pugin, each age and nation should have its own style of architecture, and Gothic, he considered, was the style that was indigenous to northern Europe, especially England. Under Pugin's guidance, the emphasis of Victorian Gothic was on function and structural 'truth' rather than on sham picturesque effects. 'What could be more absurd', Pugin wrote, 'than houses built in . . . the castellated style? Portcullises which will not lower down . . . draw-bridges which will not draw up . . . turrets so small that the most diminutive sweep could not ascend them!'[6] How he would have hated Castle House – turrets, stucco and all – although he might well have approved of the functional aspects of the building. Thus the Ecclesiologists embraced the picturesque principles of variety and intricacy, but they applied them first to the organization of space and then to other features. Churches were no longer to be square preaching boxes; appropriate spaces had also to be provided for prayer, the choir and the ministration of the sacraments. At a minimum, nave and

14

chancel should be easily distinguishable, both within and without a church. Fittings should be arranged asymmetrically and a variety of materials used.

In secular buildings, too, Pugin and the Ecclesiologists insisted that 'the exterior ought to be adapted to the internal arrangements'. In the secular buildings with which they were most concerned, vicarages, church schools and schoolhouses, they often created a building complex with the design of each structure reflecting its function. Pugin provided a model for such 'picturesque utility' in his layout of St Augustine's church and schools built adjacent to his house, The Grange, with each part treated as a separate unit, different in size and covered by a separate roof. Stefan Muthesius suggests that one of the earliest applications of this approach of the Ecclesiologists to a civic complex was the design, in 1856, by R. J. Withers of public buildings at Cardigan that combined a corn exchange, grammar school, civic offices, clock tower and market hall in a closely grouped whole.[7]

Pugin and the Ecclesiologists influenced most Victorian Gothic architects, whether they recognized it or not. For example, Seddon as late as 1872, was insisting that it was 'impossible to adapt the Greek style to our climate and wants and even that which was developed for the sunny land of Italy we may think difficult to translate into English . . .'[8] He also followed Pugin and the Ecclesiologists in objecting to neo-classical architecture where exterior appearance determined the design of the interior. He instanced Sir Gilbert Scott's controversial Foreign Office as an example of 'archituresque' considerations demanding that a five-storeyed building look three-storeyed, and so sacrificing the lighting of the interior. 'Italian regularity of the outside [had] made a hash of the requisite irregularities within.' The new housing being built in the burgeoning cities encouraged regularity, 'the vogue with vulgar and speculating builders', whose rows of terraced houses were 'models of symmetry'.[9] For Seddon, the 'agglutinative planning' of Pugin and the Ecclesiologists was much more attractive, and, in his Castle House Hotel, this is the approach he adopted.

Important though his ideas were to him, Seddon's immediate inspiration came, not from Pugin, but from John Ruskin. The Pre-Raphaelites found support for their views in the first two volumes of Ruskin's *Modern Painters* (1843 and 1846), and, once the Brotherhood was established, Ruskin became their doughtiest champion. Because of his involvement in the movement, Seddon knew Ruskin socially. For example, G. P. Boyle recalls in his diary that on 30 December 1852 he had tea with Seddon, Burges, Millais, Hunt, Ruskin and others at Rossetti's studio where they had 'sweet chestnuts and coffee, honey and hot spirits'.[10] Ruskin also admired Thomas Seddon's paintings,

particularly his *Valley of Jehosephat* (now in the Tate Gallery)[11] and, after Thomas's premature death from dysentery in Cairo in 1856, he gave the address at the memorial exhibition held at the Society of Arts during May 1857. But Ruskin was as concerned with architecture as he was with art, and his *The Seven Lamps of Architecture* (1847) shaped Seddon's architectural ideas. For Seddon, Ruskin achieved almost hagiographic status; when Seddon designed Plas Abermad for Lewis Pugh Pugh in the 1860s, he included a stained-glass rose window depicting the *Seven Lamps*.

6. 'Picturesque utility' in the design of Cardigan town hall and market by R. J. Withers in 1856.

Although Ruskin followed Pugin, both in his idealization of the 'organic' medieval communities that produced Gothic buildings, and in his antipathy to classicism, the differences between the two men were very great. Although Ruskin believed that a building should be 'strongly built', its 'highest value' was 'that it be nobly sculpted or painted'. As he noted in the second edition of the *Seven Lamps*: 'There are only two fine arts possible to the human race, sculpture and painting . . . What we call architecture is only the association of these in noble masses, or placing them in fit places; all architecture other than this is, in fact, a mere building.' Ruskin's enthusiasm for Venetian Gothic led him to advocate

16

'constructional polychromy', colour that was an integral part of a building's fabric, and this had a wide influence on Victorian architecture. For Ruskin, architectural quality therefore depended not so much on structure and the organization of internal spaces, as Pugin insisted, but on decoration. This must, in turn, be based on nature, because 'all noble ornamentation is the expression of man's delight in God's work.' These were messages to which the young Seddon was all too ready to respond.

Seddon was a founder-member of the Architectural Association, established in 1847 to encourage young architects, and which soon became something of a rival organization to the Royal Institute of British Architects. The Association was dominated by young Goths; the Institute by established neo-classicists. In 1849, Seddon was elected the Association's honorary secretary, but this did not prevent him from becoming an Associate of the RIBA three years later (and a Fellow in 1860), or from playing a prominent part in the RIBA's activities for the rest of his life. Seddon also became a member of the Ecclesiological Society and of other societies with Gothic interests, such as the short-lived Medieval Society formed in 1857.[12] The fellow architect with whom Seddon had the greatest affinity was the brilliant William Burges, who designed Cardiff Castle and rebuilt Castell Coch in the Taff Valley for the Marquis of Bute and, by so doing, created two of the most romantic buildings in Victorian Britain. Burges was Seddon's exact contemporary and, like him, was an enthusiast for the ideas and work of the Pre-Raphaelites.[13] Recalling his early days as an architect, Seddon referred to Burges as his 'kind friend . . . then my constant fellow student'.[14] If it was Ruskin who gave Seddon his enthusiasm for the architecture of Venice, it was Burges who opened his eyes to the glories of early French Gothic: 'monochrome, primitavistic, muscular, archaic'.[15] Both Burges and Seddon also discerned in Greek art and early French Gothic 'a fundamental identity of spirit'.[16]

While still a pupil, Seddon gave a number of talks to his professional colleagues at meetings of the Architectural Association. In 1851, on completing his apprenticeship, he toured the Continent, visiting France, Germany and Italy and making, as Ruskin had done before him, detailed drawings of architectural ornament everywhere he went. The following year, at the age of twenty-five, he rewrote the lectures he had given to his colleagues in the light of his European experience, and published them as *Progress in Art and Architecture* – a young architect's declaration of faith. The influence of Ruskin permeates both the style and content of Seddon's book. He attempts to replicate both Ruskin's complex syntax and the emotional intensity of his prose. The examples of ornamentation that he noted on his travels in Europe follow closely those quoted in *The Seven Lamps of Architecture*. The concern of Seddon, like Ruskin, was the appearance of buildings: rarely does he refer to structure; never to function. There are, however, fundamental differences between Seddon and Ruskin. Given Ruskin's views on the materialism and philistinism of Victorian Britain, he would never, in the title of any of his books, have suggested that progress was even possible. But Seddon was a practising architect at the beginning of his career. He was writing in 1851, the year that the Great Exhibition made manifest the triumph of industrial progress. If he was to advance professionally, Seddon had to believe that progress was 'the universal destiny of man', and that it was 'a moral duty for us to advance'.[17]

His enthusiasm for progress, however, presented Seddon, as it did his fellow Goths, with a fundamental dilemma. How could they look to a radical future while they drew their inspiration from the distant past? How could Gothic architecture be adapted, not only to the design of churches (which had been the main concern of the Ecclesiologists) but also to houses, factories and the commercial and public buildings that were proliferating in mid-Victorian Britain? Ruskin was no help in answering these questions. His holistic view that morality, economics and aesthetics were inseparably intertwined implied that true architecture could only be produced in integrated organic communities such as those he believed existed in medieval Europe. Thus, his 'Lamp of Obedience' suggested that there was no hope of advancement until architects became 'a band of freemasons as of old', and architecture was taught in schools throughout the land 'as we would teach English spelling and English grammar'. He advocated that young architects should slavishly copy Gothic forms; it was only when they were fully mature that they should be allowed 'to change or add to received forms, always within certain limits'. Furthermore, 'until a universal system of form and workmanship be everywhere adopted and enforced', Ruskin proclaimed, architecture would 'languish in the dust'. The only hope was 'the bare possibility of obtaining the consent of architects and the public to choose a style and use it universally'[18] – and this in the age of *laissez-faire*!

These views exasperated the young Seddon. He saw 'The Lamp of Obedience' as being 'fearfully quenched in gloom'. For Seddon, the days of 'feudalism and monastic compulsion' were past, so that Ruskin's social ideas were 'utterly opposed to the spirit of the age and therefore impractical'. Thus, both the attempt to re-create medieval society and the search for a universal style had to be abandoned.

The day has passed when the works of a nation should be reckoned in aggregate, and their growth described as regularly as that of a vegetable. We want neither a new nor a universal style; it were better that we knew nothing about styles; the very name of them is a bane and a hindrance to the architect, however useful to the antiquary. Let us leave it to posterity to classify our productions, and be sure that if we work simply, neither copying nor striving for singularity, we shall not then so belie the feelings of our age and country but that they must impress themselves upon our work, though we may perhaps see it not.[19]

It was certainly impossible to discover such a style through antiquarian investigation. The architect must absorb past styles and make them part of his architectural vocabulary:

Let each architect, then, shun plagiarism as a stain upon his reputation, and then all beauty is common to him; for columnar architecture, and delicacy of moulding, and precision of symmetry, are not the inalienable property of the Greek, though his several and peculiar orders are. Lofty and graceful proportion, vigorous light and shade, fairy tracery and fretted vaulting, are not a Gothic patent; though each cathedral, with its own crisp foliage and quaint imagery, and curious penetrations, and varied details, left to us throughout the length and breadth of our land as a record of the labour, and zeal, and love of their builders, is, as it were, a *sign-manual* which it is a forgery for us to repeat. The well, however, whence they drew is open to us, and we may do more and better than they, since they have shown us how, and we have not all that lesson to learn for ourselves.[20]

This eclectic approach is reflected in the examples of ornament that Seddon noted on his European tour, and drew with a skill that Ruskin must have admired. Byzantine buildings were, in his view, 'too often overlooked or undervalued', and he shared Ruskin's enthusiasm for the ornamentation of St Mark's Cathedral, Venice. He also approved the Lombard style of northern Italy and what he considered to be its extension into Germany, especially Cologne. He was attracted to the Romanesque architecture of France and its Norman equivalent in England. His major interest, however, was in Gothic ornament, in its various stages of development, that he discovered in France, Germany and Italy. He ignored 'the chaotic jumble of "monkey styles" which followed the decay of Gothic architecture, and the inundation of Europe by the torrent of the Renaissance . . .'[21] All the examples he quotes were intended as precedents; they were not to be copied. A building should not merely be an amalgam of disparate stylistic features, but, with Gothic as inspiration, the characteristics of different styles should be fused to create the architect's own style. Old College was Seddon's major attempt to realize this aspiration.

Seddon also believed that no architecture could be valid that was not based on 'nature'. Following the teaching of Ruskin and the Pre-Raphaelites, it was, in Seddon's view, essential for both artists and architects to emulate 'God's marvellous works'; to study 'the book of Nature, which is second only to that of his Revelation'. Industrialization had produced 'monotonous rows of melancholy houses' that were fast swallowing up the suburbs of all the larger towns. But it was through 'the wonders of the deep . . . the fury of the storm . . . the solitude of the desert . . . the lofty mountain peak, that the visions of the more solemn or awful import are vouchsafed to the few that seek them'.[22] Seddon correlated nature with the sublime, and sublime revelatory experiences were not possible in the suburbs. The book of Nature thus needed to be translated, a task that was the responsibility of both art and science. In materialistic Victorian Britain, progress in science had outstripped that in art. But, although science might explain the mechanisms and processes of nature, it was only art that could 'fix the most transient beam of loveliness that passes over the face of nature', and 'create beauty for herself, working with the principles she has gleaned from nature, and adding thereto the image of thought'.[23] Responding to nature was, however, more difficult for the architect than other visual artists. The materials of architecture were 'too rugged and unyielding to allow a close copying of natural forms, and thus it becomes essentially conventional'. In consequence, the architect had to involve sculptors and painters to embellish the building he was designing. Seddon interpreted Ruskin's insistence on decoration in the light of his experience of Pre-Raphaelitism. His constantly reiterated insistence on the need to integrate painting and sculpture into architecture was his most significant contribution to the Victorian architectural debate:

> Architecture embodies but the abstract principles of nature; re-creating, by means of her laws of construction and geometry, she gains sublimity by vastness, symmetry, and contrast; beauty by proportion, harmony and ornament. She builds up the polished stones of the earth into a music of visible matter, which yet is, and must remain, ever but a 'frozen music', as it has been called; out of tune with the natural melodies around, which concentrate every kind of attraction, if she avail not herself of the graces of her sister Arts. Apart from these, her means of expression are very limited, and extend not beyond the simplest of emotions of the mind, addressing but few of the sympathies of men; with no more power than the lispings of a babe, or the gestures of the dumb.[24]

Seddon had definite views on the ways in which sculpture and colour might be incorporated into a building. Architecture, being the 'framework of the whole design', should be 'predominant in all the main structural lines and features', and should be kept comparatively plain. Following Ruskin, he stated that colour should be applied to large flat surfaces. Major elements in the construction such as shafts and vaulting ribs should be kept comparatively simple and without much colouring:

> certainly they never should be striped with lines running in a vertical direction, which would destroy all their breadth, and cannot be supported by any authority in nature . . . the more natural system, as in the stems of plants

or trunks of trees, is to keep them of a single colour, which is best effected by the use of marbles – for instance, by the Purbeck marble shafts in the Early-English Gothic.

There was a possible exception, Seddon noted with a rather forced poetic flourish, when columns sprouted vaulting ribs:

> They might, perhaps, have their colour graduated as they rise or divide into their vaulting ribs, like trees into branches; such as that exquisite painting of the mountain birch in autumn, whose slender stem gleams amid the then russet wood a line of silver grey, sprayed into ebony twigs, all showered with beads of gold.

Sculpture, too, should not be coloured; 'its modelling and delicacy is seen best, or rather seen only, when left in the pure marble or stone.' Neither should statues and other ornaments be positioned so that they confused a building's outline. Hence his intense dislike of classical acroteria and of Renaissance vases stuck on parapets. Sculpture should be placed 'at the junction or intersection of the main architectural features, such as the capitals, mouldings, finials, bosses and other accessory portions, as statues in niches or crowning important points, and bas-reliefs within pediments, panels, etc.'.[25] Ornament should be derived from nature and be true to nature. The head of a beast, however abstracted, should be placed on the shoulders of a beast. A plant should never be depicted root uppermost. Thorns should not be made to bear grapes, 'nor thistles supplied with a crop of figs'. All ornament should also be related to the structure of the building of which it was a part.

> Architecture being the development of *principles* in nature, as stability, proportion, symmetry, etc., it is required of ornament, to be consistent therewith, that it should likewise embody *principles*, as lightness, elegance, growth, etc., and appear to belong to, and not be independent of, the structure. Thus it is requisite that the leaves of the capital of a column should appear to be growing therefrom, and that upwards only, and rooted firmly at the necking, not as if it were simply stuck to it or temporarily tied around it; and, further, the type of foliage they imitate must not be copied too closely, but with a considerable degree of abstraction; for as the column itself may be said to represent the tree-trunk in its general form and character of a support, while all the surface detail of the bark is omitted or merely suggested by its channelling, if the texture of the foliage be perfectly imitated, it cannot appear to be connected with the column. It is therefore essential to the nature of ornament that the copying of its type is not literal . . . [the ornamental artist's] province in design is to seize such salient points only of the natural type he may have selected, without carrying his imitation so far as to destroy the idea of the material in which it is represented, or detracting from the breadth of light and shade which its character requires.[26]

Ornament should also be adapted to the material in which it is

21

executed. Forms that are suited to stonework should not be copied in cement or wrought iron. Above all, both the structure and ornamentation of buildings should have proportion, symmetry, contrast and gradation, for these were 'principal among the qualities by which the excellence of nature is produced'.[27]

By the time that Seddon had completed his apprenticeship in 1851, he had acquired a remarkably coherent philosophy of architecture. All that he needed was the opportunity to put his ideas into practice. A Welsh family connection came to his aid. His maternal grandfather had been educated at Cowbridge Grammar School and had owned some landed property at Southerndown. This he left to his daughters of whom Seddon's mother was the eldest. As a child, John Pollard often stayed with his relations at Llanblethian and Southerndown, and he came to know the area well. As soon as he finished his apprenticeship he was invited to design and build a hotel at Southerndown 'with the view of developing the estate as a seaside resort'.[28] During 1852, while he was engaged on this project, he visited Llandaff Cathedral to look at the restoration that was then taking place. He was introduced to the cathedral architect, John Prichard, who showed him around. Prichard was ten years older than Seddon and was clearly impressed by the young Goth, who had so many metropolitan connections and such positive views about the future course of the Gothic revival. On his return to London, Seddon was 'surprised and gratified' to receive an offer of a partnership from Prichard.[29] This he accepted immediately.

John Prichard (1817–86), the son of the vicar of Llandaff Cathedral, lived in the precincts of the cathedral for much of his life. The influence of this Gothic environment on Prichard was reinforced by his being articled to A. W. N. Pugin and working on the drawings in Pugin's *Examples of Gothic Architecture*; throughout his career he called himself 'a true disciple of Pugin'. Later he was articled to Thomas Walker who was also a confirmed Gothicist. After a period in private practice, Prichard was, in 1847, appointed Llandaff's diocesan architect, responsible for the restoration of churches in Glamorgan and Monmouthshire. During the time Seddon was his partner, Prichard's most important task was the restoration of Llandaff Cathedral and, especially, his controversial rebuilding of the South Tower, with its open-work parapet and a spire that was sixty metres high.[30] Seddon's main contribution to the cathedral restoration, true to his belief about the need for architects to involve painters and sculptors, was to negotiate with his Pre-Raphaelite friends to embellish the interior. Thus Thomas Woolner, the only Pre-Raphaelite sculptor, designed a pulpit, William Morris and Edward Burne-Jones stained-glass windows, and Rossetti a sedilia and a triptych, *The Seed of David*.[31]

22

7. Perspective of Seddon's
design for Southerndown
Hotel, 1852.

Prichard had a profound influence on Seddon's development as an architect. Despite the precocious assurance Seddon had shown in his *Progress in Art and Architecture*, he had little or no experience of designing Gothic buildings. Under Donaldson's tutorship, he had concentrated on classical designs. He thus saw himself as Prichard's 'oldest pupil'. Michael Darby has pointed out the way in which, for example, Seddon's designs for the Southerndown Hotel developed, once he had met Prichard, 'to include many elements – local materials and detailing of windows, porch and doors, for example – which are reminiscent of some of Prichard's earlier designs, and were to become standard in Seddon's later gothic work'.[32] Much of the day-to-day work of the Prichard and Seddon practice was humdrum: the repair and restoration of churches (at which Seddon became very skilful, as his restoration of Llanbadarn Church shows), the building of vicarages and church schools and, occasionally, a new church. Always they had to work within stringent financial constraints. Prichard was, in the early part of their partnership, still in his thirties and Seddon in his twenties. Both were dreamers, and their dreams centred on creating a great Gothic building that would bring them international acclaim. Their contemporary, William Burges, was an even greater dreamer, but, for him, the patronage of the Marquis of Bute made even some of his most grandiose dreams come true. For Prichard and Seddon, their best hope of achieving their ambition was entering the competitions for designing public buildings that were such a feature of the life of Victorian architects.

The most important competition, during their partnership, was that in 1856 to design new Foreign and War Offices. Two hundred and eighteen designs were submitted, including a few from continental Europe and the United States. 'Reliable sources' had made it known that the government favoured a classical design, so only nineteen Gothic designs were submitted. Of these, five received minor awards, with a design by Prichard and Seddon for the War Office coming fourth.[33] This was a considerable boost for the partnership, for the winning designs were widely publicized and discussed. It was, at that time, particularly challenging to design a large public building in the Gothic style. The only precedent was the new Houses of Parliament, but, by the 1850s, they were considered to be too picturesque and were frowned upon by classicists and Goths alike.[34] However, while the competition was taking place, the Oxford Museum, designed by Deane and Woodward, was being built, and a perspective drawing of it had been published in *The Builder* in 1855.[35] It was this design that had the greatest influence on the Gothic competition submissions, including that of Prichard and Seddon. The design of the museum was directly influenced by Ruskin's writings, and followed the rejection in the 'The Lamp of Power' of picturesque outlines. Instead, Ruskin proposed that there should be a single bounding line and a rectangular façade, whereby magnitude and power were suggested by a continuous series of 'marked features' (for example, windows) 'such as the eye may be unable to number; while yet we feel, from their boldness, decision, and simplicity, that it is indeed their multitude which has embarrassed us, not any confusion or distinctness of form'. Deane and Woodward created a rectangular façade that was punctuated by regular rows of pointed windows and had a central tower. Within this regular design, they had the problem of including a chemistry laboratory and a dissecting room, both of which would produce smells. Their solution was to create two satellite buildings connected to the main block, with the laboratory being similar in its ground plan to the abbot's kitchen at Glastonbury. This was in the spirit of Pugin's insistence that different functions should have different spaces, each covered by its own roof. Prichard and Seddon followed this precedent in their War Office design. They separated the secretary of state's private and public functions by providing him with a satellite chateau which, in turn, had a satellite stable. This way of meeting

8. Perspective of the design of the University of Oxford Museum, by Benjamin Woodward and T. N. Deane, which greatly influenced Prichard and Seddon (from *The Builder*, 1855).

different needs within a unified complex was later used by Seddon in his design for the Castle House Hotel at Aberystwyth.

Contemporary critics found it difficult to discern the stylistic source of the Oxford Museum. It was variously described as Lombardo Gothic, Rhenish Gothic, Romanesque Gothic, Veronese Gothic and Early English Decorated with a strong tinge of southern Gothic.[36] This was exactly the stylistic ambiguity that Seddon was seeking in his *Progress in Art and Architecture*, and the influence of the museum design is to be seen in the massing of Prichard and Seddon's War Office building, with its rectangular façades extending on both sides of a central tower, and three rows of pointed windows and arches with polychrome decoration juxtaposed to each other and extending around the entire building. It has a fusion of styles. Prichard believed, with Seddon, that 'salvation must be sought on the continent', and the inspiration for their War Office came, as Sir John Summerson suggests, partly from Venice and partly from France.[37]

In 1858, Prichard at last obtained an important commission. John Shirley of Ettington Park, Warwickshire, invited him to provide his substantial ancestral home with an entirely new exterior – a 'wall veil' – and to add an extra storey to the garden front to create a gallery that would house a museum. This was the first attempt to give a continental Gothic style to a domestic building in Britain, and Eastlake, writing in 1870 as the first historian of the Gothic revival, was in no doubt about its significance. As in the Prichard and Seddon War Office design, the

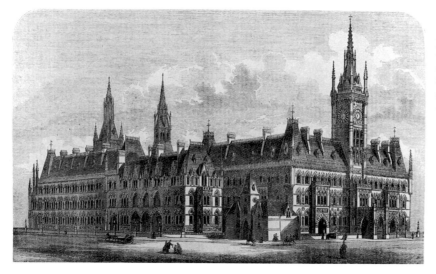

9. Prichard and Seddon's design for the War Office in London; their design was unsuccessful in the 1856 competition although they received a minor award and gained much publicity (from *Building News*, 1857).

wall veil's stylistic derivation was complex and ambiguous: a combination of English 'First Pointed', with influences from Italy and France. The ideas of Ruskin dominated the whole concept. Four different varieties and colours of stone were arranged, as Ruskin had advocated, in horizontal bands in the Italian manner, to create 'a polychromatic display of captivating delicacy and prettiness'.[39] There was also a wealth of sculptural decoration; as well as fourteen sculptured panels extolling the Shirley family's historical exploits, there were shields and crests, heads of monarchs on corbels, and full-length statues in carved niches. The building's outline, however, owes more to Pugin and the Picturesque movement than to Ruskin. As Tyack has pointed out:

> In a sense, the whole exterior of the house can be seen as a piece of sculpture. There are few flat surfaces, and the roofline is dramatic, with two contrasting towers. Prichard delighted in 'movement', projections and recessions . . .[40]

The design of Ettington Park seems to have been entirely by Prichard, with Seddon sometimes supervising the construction. Its influence on Seddon's architectural ideas was, however, crucial, as can be seen in his design of the Castle House Hotel. The exterior of the hotel is also best seen as a piece of Picturesque sculpture. In its dramatic roofline and towers, in its abundant use of sculptural ornament, in the design of the windows and in the spectacular carriage porch, it is a development of the Ettington Park design.

The Ettington Park project was, however, not a happy experience for the Prichard and Seddon partnership. Prichard saw his work at

Ettington as a major opportunity to attract more lucrative and prestigious commissions. He was concerned about every detail, and his training in Pugin's office encouraged him to make meticulous drawings of all the carvings himself. The time this took left Seddon to do all the administrative chores in their office. Prichard's costings also went awry, and completion deadlines were not met. Seddon complained of Prichard's 'unbusiness-like habits' (a comment which must have come to haunt Seddon in the light of his later experience!).[41] Prichard also became involved in the design of a house at Jerez de la Frontera for Señor Gonzalez, the sherry magnate, and this involved extended visits to Spain. All this put a great strain on the partnership. Furthermore, in 1862 Seddon got married, and he began to doubt that the practice could produce sufficient income for two people. After ten years as Prichard's 'oldest pupil', he must have felt confident enough to return to London and set up his own practice; this he did early in 1863. Prichard was distraught; he had come to rely on Seddon. In a letter to Shirley in March 1863 attempting to excuse the lack of progress at Ettington, he referred to the break-up of the partnership:

10. Prichard's design for Ettington Park, Warwickshire, the first attempt to give a continental Gothic style to a domestic building in Britain (from *Building News*, 1858).

the effects of this blow have rendered me miserable, restless and wretched, the labours of my office which used to be such Solace and Comfort to me, are now irksome, and tiresome, and I am obliged to have recourse to solitary walks in the country to soothe a grief I cannot overcome, – I verily believe my clerks think I am becoming demented, so great is the change.[42]

Seddon, however, embraced his independence with enthusiasm. His first act in setting up his new London office was to design a cabinet with shelves and drawers to hold his architectural drawings. This was no ordinary cabinet. An early example of Victorian 'medieval' furniture, it was constructed entirely of oak 'with its surface slightly polished, and profusely inlaid with root of oak and other woods of varying tones, such as ebony, purple wood, box, mahogany, oak'. The hinges and handles were 'of wrought and painted metal work'. The decoration, by Seddon, included a jocular treatment of the family's armorial bearings, with the punning motto *Non sono sed dono*. The figure of a lion rampant on the shield was drawn by William Burges. The sides had scenes with Seddon depicted as a lobster settling disputes with a client and builder shown as snakes! Seddon also commissioned William Morris's newly established firm, Messrs Morris, Marshall, Falkner and Co., to design ten panels illustrating the fine arts. The unifying theme chosen was the honeymoon of King René of Anjou, a notable medieval patron of the arts. The artists who contributed panels included Ford Madox Brown (a replica of whose design is now in the National Museum of Wales, Cardiff), Rossetti, Burne-Jones, and Valentine Prinsep. This was yet another attempt, Seddon claimed, to urge 'that in the unity of the several arts lies their power'.[43]

On his return to London, Seddon was thus drawn again into the William Morris and Pre-Raphaelite circle.[44] He and his wife became particularly friendly with the Madox Browns: 'the ladies of the Seddon family were at all times on the most cordial terms with those of the Madox Brown household.'[45] When the bachelor William Burges set up his home at Tower House, Kensington, in 1878, it was Mrs Seddon who chose the china.[46] Seddon was to design one of the first bungalow complexes in Britain, at Birchington-on-Sea, and he arranged for one of the units to be occupied by Rossetti. When Rossetti died in 1882, Seddon and Brown designed a monument to him to be placed on the embankment at Chelsea.[47] On his return to London, Seddon began to design not only 'medieval' furniture but also metalwork, stained glass, tiles and textiles. His painted furniture was, for example, well represented in the Medieval Court, arranged by William Burges, at the International Exhibition of 1862.[48] An oak escritoire with marquetry in various woods by Seddon, that was shown at the exhibition, is now in the National Museum of Wales, Cardiff. Seddon also quickly established himself amongst his fellow London architects, and in 1862 he was made honorary secretary of the RIBA. His practice prospered, although he still tended to be seen primarily as a church architect and restorer. In 1862 he entered the competition to design the St Finn Barr's Cathedral at Cork. Although Burges was the winner, the assessment of the *Building News*, at least, was that Seddon's design was probably the finest in the competition.[49] In 1863, Seddon submitted a design in the competition for the opulent Langham Hotel, to be built in Portland Place, but he was again unsuccessful. His first opportunity to be involved with a major building came, however, the following year when he was invited to design the Castle House Hotel at Aberystwyth.

3

The Castle House Hotel

When the railway line from Machynlleth to Aberystwyth was opened in 1864, a link was created with the Cambrian Line by which two trains a day travelled to and from the Midlands and London. In anticipation of a dramatic increase in tourism, plans were made to improve the promenade and seafront. By the following Easter, the Aberystwyth pier was completed, and had 7,000 customers on its opening day.[1] No one was more optimistic about the future prosperity of the town than the flamboyant and irrepressible Thomas Savin, Oswestry draper turned railway contractor, who had built the final stage of the line from Machynlleth to Aberystwyth. Mid Wales, with its unexploited mineral wealth and tourist potential, Savin insisted, had greater possibilities for development than any other part of the United Kingdom. His railway could transport an almost unlimited number of passengers; to establish itself as the Brighton of Wales, all that Aberystwyth needed was more accommodation; but it must be accommodation that provided 'people in the higher ranks' with 'those comforts and conveniences to which they were accustomed'.[2]

Savin was already preparing to cater for a boom in tourism. His grandiose plans included a string of hotels along the coast, in association with which he proposed a scheme for selling 'package' holidays that would include in the price both the train fare and the cost of boarding at his hotels. It is difficult to see how such a scheme could attract the 'higher ranks'. Indeed, David Davies of Llandinam, one of the most astute railway contractors in Britain, the builder of Barry docks and Savin's partner in constructing the Cambrian Line, was so convinced that the scheme would fail that he extricated himself from the partnership.[3] Undeterred, Savin went on to construct a hotel at Borth and to make plans for other hotels at Towyn and Aberdovey. He bought Castle House as his Aberystwyth residence, but with the intention of enlarging it into a hotel. For these projects, he engaged Seddon as his architect.

Initially, Savin's plans for his Aberystwyth hotel were modest enough.

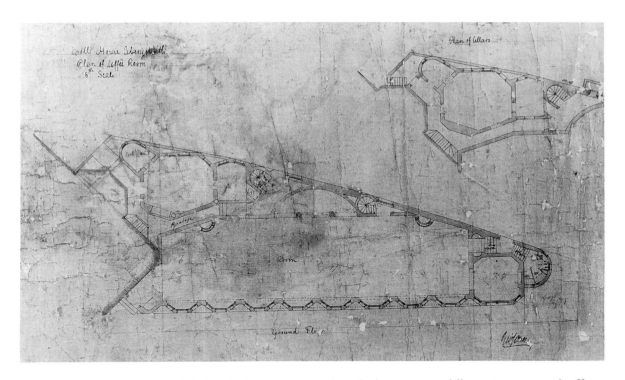

11. Seddon's plan for the 'coffee room' (or restaurant) for the Castle House Hotel, 1864.

All that Seddon was asked to design was a public restaurant, or 'coffee room', attached to the south side of Castle House. This was to have a flat roof that could be used as a promenade. Seddon recalls the way in which Savin insisted that he prepare a sketch-plan of the proposed restaurant the day he made his initial visit to the site. This Savin approved that evening, and asked Seddon to supervise the laying of the foundations the following morning![4] It was now late spring, and Savin hoped that the restaurant would be ready for the 1865 season. Seddon returned to London to prepare working drawings. Before he had time to do so, he received further instructions from Savin to provide a suite of bedrooms above the restaurant and for a larger kitchen at the rear. More ominously, he was informed that, as the materials that he had ordered could not be obtained in time, the building was to be constructed by Savin's workmen in ordinary brickwork, which was then to be covered in cement. Seddon, with his Ruskinian belief in truth to materials, must have been aghast. Even so, by the end of July, Seddon had prepared detailed plans, and the *Aberystwyth Observer* was able to report on 6 August that Savin had 'just commenced to make great additions to his Castle-House, his residence in this town'. These would 'render the castle an imposing and spacious edifice', with 'a most picturesque appearance'.[5] Paradoxically, the most picturesque aspect of the new wing arose from the change in building materials ordered by Savin.

31

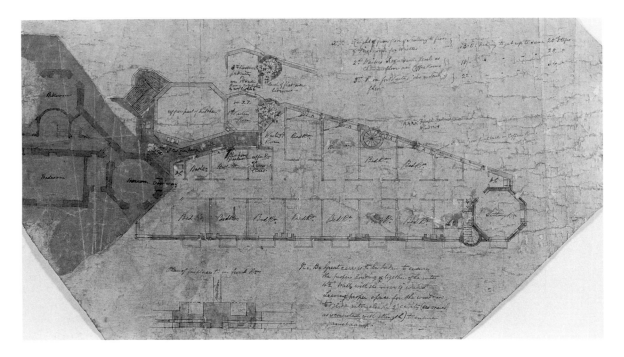

Seddon now provided the upper storey with a timber frame that had panels filled in with $4\frac{1}{2}$-inch brickwork, covered with Portland cement and decorated with incised and coloured lines and patterns. This, the *Building News* suggested rather fancifully, was in the tradition of 'old-fashioned timber construction of the West of England and Wales'.[6] Inside, a thicker brick wall was built with a cavity between it and the timber frame. This made possible the promenade above. To alleviate the monotony of the flat roof-line, Seddon added an octagonal tower, with spire, towards the southern end of the wing, and two minor towers above the staircases to the roof promenade. At Ettington, Eastlake had noted that even the chimneys were 'invested with a picturesque character which is all their own, and none the less admirable for their originality'.[7] This was also true of the chimneys Seddon created for the Castle House wing. Having been forced to use brick and cement for the rest of the wing, Seddon, for the chimney stacks, used Ransome's patent stone which could be moulded into various shapes.[8]

The restaurant, which occupied the whole of the ground floor, had eight polygonal bay windows facing the sea. On the opposite side there was a bar in a semi-circular recess that was divided from the main room by an arcade of three arches upon marble columns. The whole area was heated by two semi-circular hooded fireplaces that were similar to the fireplaces that still exist in the Seddon Room in Old College, and the ceiling had elaborate plasterwork. At its southern end, the restaurant

12. The first floor, above the coffee room, of the Castle House Hotel was to have fourteen bedrooms.

32

opened to a polygonal room in the tower which increased the length of the dining room from 96 feet to 115 feet. The entrance was in a sheltered position behind this room. The kitchen, like the laboratory at the Oxford Museum, was an octagonal extension, separate from the rest of the building. To provide more room, the kitchen was housed in the basement, and connected to the ground floor by a lift and two staircases. The kitchen ceiling then rose to fifty feet and was ventilated by an open roof and lantern. Seddon left it to the Sheffield firm of Longden to provide the kitchen fittings and make what use they thought appropriate of the space he had created.

On the first floor, there were some fourteen bedrooms, with the eight rooms facing the sea having wooden balconies floored with encaustic tiles. There were two bathrooms and two WCs. In the tower, at the southern end, there was an octagonal sitting-room, with a writing closet in the adjoining turret. This room had two balconies. Doorways were cut between the ground and first floors of the wing and Castle House. The upper sashes of all the windows in the wing had ornamental glass and circular panes that echoed the circular windows in the Nash house. The lower sashes were filled with plate glass to give clearer visibility. An impression of the bay windows is given by the longitudinal section of the coffee room prepared by Seddon.

Given the constraints of the dagger-shaped site, the juxtaposition of the wing to Nash's picturesque house, Savin's insistence on a flat roof, as well as the speed with which he had to work, Seddon's design was remarkably innovative. This was the first time that, independent of Prichard, he had applied his stylistic eclecticism to a large building. Inevitably, he remained influenced by the designs for the Oxford Museum, the War Office and Ettington Park. The façade followed the Oxford Museum in the simplicity of its silhouette. This was Venetian in inspiration, as were other features, such as the parapet, the balconies and ground-floor windows, which were so deeply set that they gave the impression of being an arcade. This was the 'marked feature' that helped to give the wing its sublimity. Seddon also attempted to marry the wing to the house by making the towers and kitchen octagons. As in the Oxford Museum and War Office designs, a focal point was provided by a tower, but sited towards the southern end of the building rather than at the centre. The unhappiest feature of Seddon's design was the timber construction of the first floor, and the use of brick covered in cement for the rest of the building. These features were only included because Savin thwarted Seddon's original design. Given the way in which temporary buildings tend to become permanent, Seddon could not have been much comforted in knowing that the wing had a 'supposed comparatively temporary purpose'. He must have begun to question his

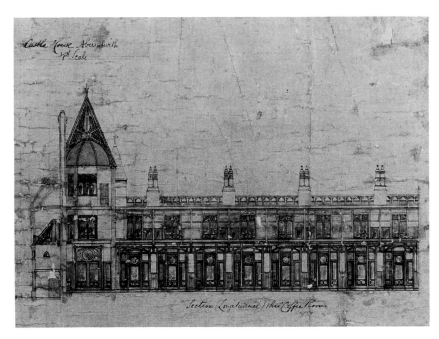

13. Longitudinal section of the coffee room and first floor of Castle House Hotel.

14. The back elevation of the coffee room.

34

rejection of Ruskin's belief that it was impossible to create architecture of distinction in a materialistic entrepreneurial society. Not surprisingly, there is no record of him building in this way again.

Seddon's connection with Savin and Aberystwyth was, however, far from over. In the autumn of 1864, he was again sent for by Savin and instructed to continue 'with all possible speed' with a still larger wing on the northern side of Castle House. Savin was now determined to build a hotel that was even grander than the Queen's Hotel, with its eighty-three bedrooms, that was being constructed by the rival Hafod Hotel Company a short distance along the promenade. The *Aberystwyth Observer* was convinced that he would succeed; the Castle House Hotel would 'not only be the finest in Wales, but, in architectural pretensions [would] rival the finest hotels in England'.[9] With the expansion of the railways in the 1860s, new hotels proliferated throughout Britain. Many were large and ostentatious, being modelled on the grand hotels established in the early nineteenth century in the United States. These had a lavish provision of public rooms and also a number of private suites to meet the needs of permanent residents. This pattern was followed by the best London hotels. Indeed, Brown's Hotel in Dover Street, which opened in 1837, only had suites.[10] Hotels in the provinces, such as the Queen's Hotel, Cheltenham (1836–8), that catered for families on holiday, also had a number of suites, as did the hotels at railway termini built as status symbols by the railway companies or their subsidiaries. At the Great Western Hotel (1851–2) at Paddington, for example, the accommodation varied from large apartments on the first floor, with private WC, at the cost of 22s. 6d. per day, to small bedrooms on the fourth floor at 1s. 6d.[11] Seddon had entered the competition for the grandest sixties London Hotel, the Langham, Portland Place, where the winning design by John Giles provided beds for 400 people, and included 36 sitting- and drawing-rooms.[12]

At Aberystwyth, too, the north wing that Savin and Seddon planned 'was to include a suite of public drawing-rooms, a public bar and billiard rooms, with numerous private sitting-rooms and bedrooms'. The design was 'to afford accommodation for a large number of persons on the American system of living in common, while the original Castle House could be retained for the more private use of a single family, as also other private apartments to be provided, and yet all served from the same kitchen and waiting department'. Seddon was now supplied with better working materials than when building the south wing. The stone used for the walling was a cinnamon-coloured Permo-Triassic sandstone from the Greenshill Quarry near Clive, between Shrewsbury and Wem in Shropshire.[13] For the dressings, 'the best description of Bath stone' was used. The shafts of the columns, which acted as mullions for all the windows, were of a 'delicate, bluish tinted sandstone from Hanam near Bristol', although, at the back of the building, the mullions were alternately of a red conglomerate from Radyr near Cardiff. This stone, being very hard, was also used for the steps. Initially, the north wing was to have three storeys, but, as the building proceeded, so Savin became ever more ambitious, and he ordered the height to be increased to at least six storeys. This made some of the internal courts appear small in relation to the building's height. Seddon bewailed the problems which Savin's unbridled ambition caused him:

> I had some difficulty under the circumstances in controlling the massing of the buildings so that they might group satisfactorily as a whole; the more so, as from the haste with which I was obliged to press on and keep 500 men in full employment, I was never able to make any complete drawings. A rough wooden model was all that I could prepare for general guidance, with the requisite working drawings for details as they were required.

Such frenetic activity was only possible because Savin had his own work-force who were supervised by a local architect, George Jones. In his anxiety to complete the building, Savin made no attempt to control the cost; Seddon's creativity was unfettered; his imagination could run riot. Patently, Seddon's aim was not to create a unified structure, but a group of buildings in the style of the Ecclesiologists, as exemplified by the civic centre at Cardigan. There was no intention, at that time, of razing Castle House, while the southern wing, with all its peculiarities, was already built. Ultimately, Seddon intended to replace Castle House, but, even then, as his 1865 plan shows, the ground-plan was to be retained, but with Nash's towers transformed into picturesque spires. Seddon's task was made even more difficult because the long and irregular site forced him to place his buildings in a row. The site did, however, have one advantage: unlike most Victorian town buildings, the hotel could be viewed from all sides, and not from the front only; it could be designed in the round.

In order to provide convenient access to both the northern and southern parts of the complex, Seddon placed the main entrance, reception, services, bar, main staircase, lift, servants' staircase, billiard room and smoking room together, next to Castle House. The main entrance was on the sheltered town side, and approached through a carriage porch. This would have been almost a replica of the Ettington carriage porch as initially designed, but for the difficulty of negotiating the angle of Castle House. Seddon's response to this problem was to create a triangular porch which, with its vaulted and ribbed interior, was one of the most individual and striking features of the building. Approaching the carriage porch, guests could not but also be impressed

Castle Hotel, Aberystwith.

JOHN P. SEDDON.
Architect
12 Park Street
Westminster S.W.

15. Elevation from the King Street side and plan of the Castle House Hotel as designed originally by Seddon.

by the sublime thickness of the walls and the massive double tower that confronted them. Immediately on entering the hotel, they would experience the dramatic vista, through a colonnade of banded columns, to the bar beyond. Such columns are found throughout the north wing, not only for supporting arches and vaulting, but also as mullions and even as ornamentation for the chimneys; they are the leitmotiv of the building. J. Coates Carter, who became Seddon's partner in the 1880s, traces Seddon's use of columns to his early classical training with Donaldson. Seddon, he suggests, made this columnar form of Gothic his own; it was 'an absolutely original form, though owing something also to his love and study of Venetian Gothic, but as distinct from the one as from the other in minor details and sentiment'.[14]

The ceiling of the bar was of wood and was vaulted. This was the lower part of a 'double framed' floor that was intended to give added rigidity to the billiard room above, but it was in reality merely decorative – a picturesque feature of which Gothic purists would have strongly disapproved. Seddon used the same type of vaulting in the sitting- and drawing-rooms, and intended to do so in the large drawing-room, but this was never completed. The bar was to be heated by the two

37

16. The colonnade of banded columns in the interior of the main entrance of the hotel.

17. The main staircase and ceiling.

semicircular hooded fireplaces that can be seen in the Seddon Room today. The bar area opened directly to the main staircase and lift (surely one of the few lifts in the country entered through Gothic arches), and then to the main corridor of the new north wing. The main staircase is one of the most impressive features of the building. Approached through double-banded columns, it leads, first, to a large and striking curved Gothic window, with columnar mullions each of which has four bands, and then continues right and left round two more columns that support vaulting which is richly carved with corbels depicting formalized heads. In what he called 'a segmented aspidal projection' from the window, Seddon intended placing a small fountain. The hole from which the jet of water was to emerge can still be seen.

18. The Gothic window on the main staircase.

A separate staircase led to the smoking and billiard rooms, – areas that were obviously intended to be the exclusive preserve of the hotel's male customers. The smoking-room was situated above the main entrance in the area that united the Nash house with the main building. It then extended up a short staircase into a delightful room, triform in plan, that was situated in the major tower over the staircase vaulting. The whole of this area has a wide view over Laura Place. The adjacent billiard room was very grand; it was oval, with the exterior wall projecting outwards above the bar and carried by arches supported by buttresses between the bar windows. The room, 48 feet by 24 feet, provided space for three full-size billiard tables, with the curved recesses on each side providing additional space for spectators. The recesses were divided off by arcades of three arches resting upon triple groups of columns.

Having accepted that he was creating a building complex rather than a single structure, Seddon, in the tradition of Pugin, housed the areas discussed above in what was virtually a separate building. This part of the hotel, which provided a focus for the whole complex, is one of the

19. The front exterior of the Seddon Room, adjoining the central block.

40

most original designs in Victorian architecture. As at Ettington, it is best considered as a piece of sculpture. Its great curved front mirrored the front of the adjacent Castle House; its steeply pitched roof, pierced with two conical spires, is reminiscent of a French Renaissance chateau; the three deeply set ground-floor windows evoke the entrance to a French Gothic cathedral. Together, they provide a wealth of abstract forms which a twentieth-century sculptor might envy.[15] The town side of the building is equally dramatic. Above the main staircase, there rises a double tower, designed to be as high as ten storeys. The larger tower houses the main staircase and a number of rooms; the smaller tower the servants' staircase. The ground-plan of the two towers taken together is an irregular trefoil. From the top of the larger tower it might be possible, at last, to see 'the monarch Snowdon'. It was intended, also, to place an observatory on the top, but this never materialized. By creating this central block, with its massive curved front and lofty towers, Seddon had placed next to Nash's picturesque house a sublime structure. More cynically, this part of the hotel complex could be seen as a gigantic and

20. The back exterior of the central block, showing the triangular carriage porch and double tower.

41

29. Seddon's perspective of the college in 1871, showing how he hoped the college would look once money became available to complete the building.

Even the repair and maintenance of the existing structure was too much for the committee's resources. There were moves to rent the building for £150 a year to the British Schools Society for use as a women's teacher-training college. As a last resort, it was even suggested that the building be sold.[4] In 1872, however, the committee set aside all caution and appointed the college's first principal, Thomas Charles Edwards, supported by a small staff of two professors (classics and natural science) and a registrar-cum-librarian. In October the college opened with twenty-six students, but their numbers increased to sixty-two during the session. The college was desperately poor; although there were plenty of bedrooms available, it was impossible to board the students because there was not enough money to buy bedroom furniture; they had to live in lodgings in the town.[5] However, by the third session, rooms were provided in the college for a professor and ten students.[6]

By October 1874, too, enough money had been collected to clear the college's outstanding debts. In the same year, a body of Trustees, a Court of Governors and a Council were established. The governors hoped to create an endowment fund of £50,000 and a nation-wide campaign of house-to-house and chapel collections was launched. As many as 70,000 people contributed, but individual sums were small. During 1874, for example, a total of only some £3,100 was raised in this way.[7] But the college could now at least begin to think about completing the building. The northern end, in particular, in its forlorn and unfinished state was, the principal had to admit, 'an eyesore for all the lovers of the beautiful'.[8] The principal's wife, however, found a use for the waste ground; as Sir John Lloyd was later to recall, it became 'sacred to Mrs Edwards's hens'. For the 'athletic', it was also an entry into the building after hours.[9]

Seddon was asked for a statement, with an estimate of cost, of how the north end might be completed, and also for an estimate of the cost of completing the great central tower. It was the governors' intention to do no more than finish the external walls and windows, with the internal work being deferred until additional rooms were required. This was an approach that suited Seddon. He proposed that two halls be created, one over the other, for which 'many uses in connection with the College, or even independent uses could be found, such as libraries, museums, assembly halls, chapels etc.'. Seddon estimated that rebuilding the external walls and constructing a tower at the north-west angle of the building, would cost £5,000. The completion of the great tower would cost a further £1,500.[10]

Such sums would be difficult to obtain from voluntary subscriptions, and no real progress could be made without a government grant. But this would set a precedent that would be seized upon by universities throughout the kingdom; as a result, even the most intense pressure from the college's supporters brought no response from the Treasury. The college continued to nurse the vain hope that the government might be prepared to contribute a non-recurrent grant of some £5,000 toward its building fund, and another £5,000 might be obtained from voluntary subscriptions. J. Ffoulkes Roberts, a Machynlleth-born Manchester business man, a close friend of T. C. Edwards and a college vice-president, took a particular interest in building matters, and in 1877 he pledged that the college's Manchester local committee would be responsible for raising the £5,000. But times were hard even for Manchester business men; they decided that, 'because of the exceptional depressed state of trade', it would be inappropriate to launch an appeal.[11] The slump affected Aberystwyth, too; by 1879, matters became so bad that the college was facing bankruptcy. There was now concern throughout Wales and, in the general election that took place in 1880, almost every candidate pledged to press the government to give financial support to higher education in Wales. One of Gladstone's first acts on returning to office after his resounding election victory was to appoint a committee under the chairmanship of Lord Aberdare to consider the whole question of higher and 'intermediate' education in Wales.[12] The committee's main conclusion in relation to higher education was that the geography of Wales was such that there was a need for a college both in the north and in the south. The northern college might remain at Aberystwyth or could be moved to either Bangor or Caernarfon. Responding to the Report, the government promised an annual grant of £4,000 to both the northern and southern colleges. Cardiff was the obvious site for the college in the south and, after much controversy, Bangor, and not Aberystwyth, was chosen as the site for the northern college. There then followed considerable agitation to retain Aberystwyth as a third college. In the end, the government compromised and, in June 1884, the Treasury agreed to a grant of £2,500 to Aberystwyth on condition that £1,000 was raised by private subscription.

Indications of support from both Wales and Whitehall encouraged the college Council to contemplate a new building programme. In October 1884, a building committee was established, and the principal was asked to visit other colleges 'in order to obtain information bearing on the proposed completion of the college buildings and appliances'.[13] As a result T. C. Edwards visited Cambridge (where he also gave a couple of sermons). More surprisingly, he also approached a London architect with the splendid Dickensian name of Aldwinckle to complete the building. The firm of Szlumper and Aldwinckle had, in 1872, designed the Aberystwyth Board School in Alexandra Road, one of the first board schools to be built in Wales, and one of the last to be conceived in a Gothic style.[14] The principal's initiative gave J. Ffoulkes Roberts 'real joy'. As he noted to Edwards: 'I was delighted to find you had your eye on a man likely to suit you as an architect without going to Mr Seddon who I was afraid would have landed us in considerable cost.'[15] That such a decision could be made by 'educated men' was in the view of *The Builder* 'quite incomprehensible'. Seddon's building was 'a very fine and original architectural conception', and that he should have waited for so many years in vain to complete it, was an injustice to which *The Builder* objected 'very strongly'.[16] In January 1885 Seddon took the matter up himself. He wrote to the college Council complaining that, since 1875, when he prepared plans for completing the north wing, he had been waiting patiently for the college to obtain the means to carry them out. No other architect was in the position he was in to do the work 'with economy'. It was only he who knew best 'how to utilize to advantage all the unfinished portion of the structure, at the same time preserving the architectural effect of the whole'. Crucially, he still held the commission from the college, his 1875 plans having been retained without any payment being made. 'Under these circumstances', he concluded, 'no other architect should have been consulted, or should have accepted a commission, until I had been settled with; the matter therefore remains open for your consideration.'[17]

Sensing a legal wrangle, the Council hurriedly looked up their earlier minutes and, after 'a lengthy conversation', decided that a three-man delegation, Lord Aberdare, Stuart Rendel and Lewis Morris, should meet Seddon to try to clear the matter up.[18] At this meeting Seddon agreed to accept 50 guineas for the work that he had done in the 1870s, on the understanding that several of his drawings be retained by the college. He also undertook to prepare another set of drawings and estimates to meet new instructions given by the college. For these he agreed to a fee of 10 guineas if he were then appointed the architect and 20 guineas if he were not. The Council gave a similar commission to Aldwinckle.[19] In the event, it was Seddon's designs that the Council approved and, at a meeting on 9 June, he was appointed as the architect to complete the north wing.

30. The college immediately after the fire of 1885, which gutted the whole of the building north of the Nash house.

Tragically, almost before Seddon had begun to prepare detailed plans, fate intervened. During the night of the 8/9 July 1885, a fire broke out in the chemistry laboratory on the fifth floor of the King Street side of the north wing. Driven by a high wind, this spread across the well that divided the wing from north to south, and then to the central block, destroying the library that was, at that time, housed in the former billiard room. The force of the fire was such that, tragically, three of the fire-fighters were killed and a number injured. The whole of the building north of the Nash house was gutted; only the outer walls and the uncompleted towers remained.[20] It was a sad paradox that the only parts of the building to be saved were the Nash house, which it was planned to replace, and the south wing which, when it was built in 1864, Seddon hoped would have only a short life. 'It looked for all the world', Dr Ellis concludes, 'as if the elements had conspired together to achieve the end of Aberystwyth college, something that years of disappointment, grinding poverty, the contempt of the well-to-do, and the indifference of a succession of not especially helpful governments had failed to do.'[21] Fortunately, as Dr Ellis has shown, this proved not to be so. The college building had become a potent national symbol. Viriamu Jones, the principal of the University College, Cardiff, when writing to sympathize with T. C. Edwards about the college's loss (though he addressed his letter to the 'University College of Mid-Wales'), recognized that 'the old building was from the point of view of Welsh Education historic and its destruction will be felt and regretted by every Welshman'.[22] Others were even more forceful. One correspondent noted that working people throughout Wales cherished for Aberystwyth 'a kind of personal and proprietary sentiment'.

When they heard the news of the fire, they went back in memory to those Sunday evenings ten or twelve years ago when in their little Bethels they contributed their crowns, half-crowns and shillings towards the *first* Welsh university college, and they felt as if some calamity had befallen themselves ... Facts like these unmistakably attest the depth and fervour of the national feeling on behalf of our national college *par excellence*.[23]

Even the government now became conscious of the affection with which the college was held by the Welsh people, and increased its grant to £4,000 per annum, putting Aberystwyth on a par with the colleges at Bangor and Cardiff. A new campaign was initiated to establish a building fund and this, with the £10,000 obtained from the insurance of the existing building, made possible a more ambitious building programme.

Seddon rushed to Aberystwyth on the day of the fire and, five days later, wrote to the college Council estimating that the damage amounted to £20,000.[24] But, determined to save his building, he now saw an opportunity to remodel the whole of the north wing, and replace most of the smaller apartments with the larger class-rooms that the college so badly needed. He estimated that this could be done at a cost of £15,000 (excluding the northern end) and submitted a complete set of plans, elevations and sections showing how the modifications might be made.[25] Members of the Council were, however, divided as to whether it was preferable to have an entirely new building on a new site, or to restore the old. Seddon was asked to compare the cost of restoration with that of erecting a new structure. Some 1,700,000 cubic feet were required. Seddon considered that seven pence a cubic foot would be sufficient for the type of building that was being envisaged, giving a cost of £52,000. From this £5,000, the site value of the existing building, should be deducted. But if the existing building were retained, it could be restored, and the northern end completed, at six pence a cubic foot, giving a total cost of £25,670.[26]

A new building on an open site would, however, have the advantage of being purpose-built and capable of extension as student numbers grew. In any case, the Building Committee, knowing the intensity of Seddon's desire to see his building completed, must have been suspicious of his costings. It was, therefore, decided to hold an architectural competition, with three prizes of £100, £50 and £25, for the design of a new building of some 16,000 square feet and of 'a simple but solid character, without great ornamental features or detail'. Inevitably, the college Council added that they would 'be largely guided in their selection of designs by considerations of economy'.[27]

One of the difficulties that the committee had in providing the competitors with a brief was that it had no site in mind. Sir Pryse Pryse of Gogerddan owned a number of fields on the outskirts of Aberystwyth, but he insisted that the college choose a site before he would quote a price. The brief, therefore, merely stated that allowance

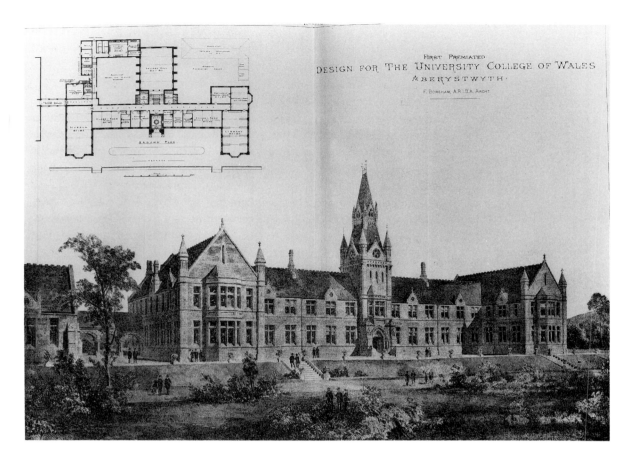

was to be made for a sloping site! *The Builder*, always a staunch supporter of Seddon, pointed to the ludicrousness of this situation:

> No building can be satisfactorily designed in this way, and we cannot help adding that we think the Council must have an inadequate idea of Mr Seddon's very exceptional abilities if they expect to get anything better than he could give them by throwing him over a second time for this kind of blind competition for a building without a site.[29]

The first prize in the competition was won by a London architect, Frederick Boreham, for a cost-conscious design that provided the kind of basic accommodation that was soon to be found in intermediate schools throughout Wales – except for the elaborate central tower. At a meeting of the college Council on 31 May 1886, when the name of the winner was announced, a letter from Seddon was read out. This pointed out that the comparison that the Council had asked him to make between the costs of a new building and those of renovation of the old stipulated far more space than that laid down in the competition brief. He was prepared to make an estimate that would meet the new

31. Perspective of the design by Frederick Boreham which won the college's competition in 1886 for a cost-conscious, functional building to house the college on a new site. This design was eventually abandoned in favour of Seddon's adaptation of the original building.

58

'diminished requirements', and show that they could be provided within the old building, leaving a large amount of space for future developments, and that this could be done in half the time needed to construct a new building on a new site.

By this time the Council was aware of the intensity of the support for the existing building from students, past and present, as well as those who might subscribe to a building fund. The students, in particular, did not want to exchange a building in the centre of the town for a non-residential college situated up a steep hill somewhere on the outskirts. As they pointed out in a memorial to the Council, they were all attached to the existing building, 'adjacent to the fine ground of the old castle' and overlooking 'the changeful and beautiful waters of Cardigan Bay'. Above all, they did not wish to lose 'the noble porch and commanding towers, which [gave] the pile an aspect of strength and grandeur'.[30]

For the Council, it was the relative cost of the two schemes that was decisive. An architect member, Lewis Angell, had estimated that, at seven pence a cubic foot, the building designed by Boreham would cost £23,875. In order for a valid comparison to be made, Seddon was given a fortnight to prepare and cost new plans.[31] These attempted to show that all the college requirements could be amply met in the existing building, leaving considerable additional space that would meet the college's probable needs for a long time to come, and all at a cost of at the most £17,500. As a result, 'a far nobler building would thus be retained and completed at a cost more than one-third less than must be otherwise expended upon a new one of comparatively inferior pretensions and smaller scale.'[32]

Another report had been compiled for the Council which suggested that, of the two most eligible sites for a new college, one had an incline of 1 in 5, and the other 1 in 6. This would make them undesirable as sites and would considerably increase the building costs. The total cost of a new building, the Council calculated, would thus not be less than £28,000. As the building fund stood at some £10,000, with promises of a further £5,000, the only decision that the Council could come to was that the existing building be reconstructed. It was agreed that Seddon should go ahead and prepare detailed plans but that, if a tender could not be obtained for less than £17,500, Seddon would have to forego his commission of $2\frac{1}{2}$ per cent.[33]

Seddon proposed that the whole structure be remodelled as a two-storey building, thus returning to his initial design before Savin insisted that the northern wing be six storeys. As it was intended that in the future students would not be resident, the arts were to be housed in the northern wing, and science in the southern wing, divided from each other by the principal's house. The whole would 'form one continuous

range of plain and substantial, but picturesque, buildings of fireproof construction, having an ample provision of light and air to every portion'.[34] The most inspired change was to clear the space at the centre of the north wing that, in the original hotel, had been occupied by rooms looking into the internal well, and create a great central corridor or quadrangle that was inspired by Seddon's Law Courts design. This had access to the rooms on the King Street side by three newly created staircases. On the seaward side there was to be an impressive central staircase that led not only to rooms on the western side of the building but also to a balcony that ran round the quadrangle and gave access to the library and all first-floor rooms.

It was intended that the bar area of the original hotel would house the college museum which would then overflow into the quadrangle. The former billiard-room was, appropriately, to be the men students' common-room, while the former smoking-room, with its separate staircase opposite the porter's lodge, was initially intended to be the women's common-room. The great drawing-room would become the college hall with a library above, 'in a quiet retired position with ample lights'. Seddon proposed to remove the first-floor timber frame and roof from the science wing, and reconstruct both floors with fireproof walling of local hard stone with all the dressings in a stone able to resist sea air. In all, the reconstruction would take eighteen months.[35]

Seddon prepared a perspective drawing of his reconstructed building.

32. Seddon's perspective of 1886 of the proposed reconstruction of the college building.

This shows the effect of the reduction in the height of the north wing. Compared with the 1870–1 elevation, the examination hall and library block at the north end was now lower, so that its gable was below the height of the rest of the wing. Seddon still hoped to heighten the central tower so that it could house a telescope. He again planned, ultimately, to replace Castle House, but now with a more functional, if less attractive, block than that which he had proposed in 1870–1. This was intended as a 'grand central hall' if such were required, or, otherwise, as an extension of the science accommodation.[36] When he came to make a detailed survey of the outer walls of the north wing, he realized that they had been less affected by the fire than he had thought initially. During the summer, too, a number of suggestions were made to him for additional rooms and facilities, and these demanded some extra 7,000 square feet. As a result he decided to retain the north wing in its entirety. This not only made it possible for him to meet all immediate demands, but also to have considerable space in reserve for future use. Although the amount of space was now increased from the 23,185 square feet originally stipulated, to 49,316 square feet, the adaptation could still be made, Seddon believed, for £17,500. 'Had such a building to be created *de novo*,' he once again reminded the Council, 'there can be no question that it would take double the present estimated amount, and double the time, to be carried into execution.'[37] In the event, the lowest tender, by the London firm of S. Balham and Co., was for £17,900. However, the excess of £400 could, in Seddon's view, be easily recouped from the sale of materials which were not required in the reconstruction.[38] This the Council was prepared to accept, but, still wary of Seddon's profligacy, it resolved that the Building Committee's sanction must be obtained for all extras above £20. J. Ffoulkes Roberts, in particular, remained suspicious of Seddon. As early as August 1886, he entreated the principal to ensure that the plans were 'fully mature' before the contracts were made 'so as to avoid alterations of which Mr Seddon will get a good deal of pickings'.[39] This was a grossly unjust comment. If Seddon had a fault it was, as Carter later noted, that his enthusiasm for his art sometimes carried him 'away from the mere utilities of life'.[40] It was libellous to suggest that he was interested in 'pickings'. Roberts, with his brash Manchester business background, and Seddon, imbued with the ethics of the William Morris circle, did not speak the same language. The Balham tender was accepted on 22 February 1887 and the clearing of the site began almost immediately.

After the fire, the college was housed in rented premises around Aberystwyth, with the the arts subjects being taught in the Queen's Hotel. Temporary science laboratories were difficult to provide. When rebuilding the college it was decided, therefore, to give priority to the science wing. The whole wing was razed to the ground, with only the foundations and basement remaining. Seddon must have been delighted to see the ugly 'roof apartment', the timber framing and walls of brick faced with concrete come down. He could begin this part of the building *de novo*. Although over twenty years had elapsed since he designed the Castle House Hotel, Seddon remained true to his belief that, with Gothic as inspiration, the architect should create his own style. Now, however, the basis of his eclecticism was no longer a mixture of Venetian and French; Venetian Gothic was abandoned in favour of thirteenth-century France; the influence of Burges had triumphed over Ruskin. Gone were the picturesque chimneys, the decorative parapet, balconies and deep-set ground-floor windows. Instead there was a steeply pitched roof and a tower with a conical spire, flanked by an oriel turret with a conical spirelet, which was repeated at the northern end of the wing. (This latter turret was removed when Castle House was replaced in the 1890s.) All these were features reminiscent of Burges's Castell Coch. The windows on the first floor had, typically for Seddon, columns as mullions, but the design of the ground-floor windows, although Gothic in inspiration, was new to him. The ground-plan of the wing remained that of the hotel, although the internal space was now divided into laboratories, lecture rooms and the like, with chemistry being housed on the ground floor and botany and physics on the first floor. The plan of the hotel's circular kitchen was also retained, but this became a lecture theatre. Although Seddon, in order to economize, initially intended to build the science wing of local stone, he later decided to use sandstone from the Greenshill quarries that matched the rest of the building.[41] At this early stage, he felt sure that he could make savings elsewhere and keep within his estimate.

The new wing's elevation was impressively clean-cut. There was a minimum of sculptural decoration; the money available allowed little else. There was the occasional gargoyle to relieve the monotony of the back of the building, and future scientists, on entering the main doorway, could be inspired by the serpent of 'darkness' being strangled by the hand of 'light', and that of 'error' by 'science'. The most spectacular, and original, decoration of the south wing was, however, the large and colourful mosaic on its southern tip that Seddon provided at his own expense. This was his most ambitious attempt to incorporate

33. The new science block after reconstruction, with the original Castle House in the centre of the building.

an example of two-dimensional art into a building. The mosaic was designed by C. F. A. Voysey (1857–1941), a leading member of the Arts and Crafts movement who pushed his designs for furniture, fabrics and wallpapers beyond those of William Morris so that they became an inspiration for art nouveau. Voysey also revolutionized house design, and his white stuccoed houses, with their steeply pitched roofs, horizontal fenestration and massive chimney stacks, were extensively copied in both Britain and continental Europe. He became one of the most influential architects and designers of the twentieth century. Voysey was articled to Seddon from 1873 to 1878, but then continued to work for him for a further year. Seddon and Voysey got on very well. Seddon introduced his pupil to the writings of Pugin, and instilled in him the importance of the architect finding his own voice. While still a pupil, Voysey painted life-size pictures of angels in a church that Seddon was designing.[42] So it was that, some seven years after he had completed his apprenticeship, Voysey was invited by Seddon to design the Aberystwyth murals.

Voysey created a triptych in the Renaissance tradition, but the central panel depicted a representation, not of Christ or of the Virgin and

34. The triptych on the turret of the south wing, designed by C. F. A. Voysey, depicting Science flanked by figures presenting a locomotive and a ship, symbols of modern engineering.

Child, but of Science with stars around his head and a globe at his side, symbols respectively of the heavens and the earth. On his lap, there is a book with a drawing of a skull signifying the study of 'man' and a triangle representing 'mathematics', the basis of all scientific knowledge. In the left panel, a kneeling male figure holds a locomotive and on the right an 'epicene' figure holds a ship, powered partly by steam and partly by sail. The iconography is thus clear: the 'donors' in the side panels are presenting 'Science' with examples of modern engineering that ultimately depended on the knowledge of man, the world and the universe that had been gained by the pure scientists. Without the pursuit of free untrammelled enquiry, the transition from sail to steam would not have been possible. Applied science must thus genuflect to pure science: a message that is as pertinent for universities today as it was in the late nineteenth century.

Originally, both the design and iconography of the mural were more complex. In the first design, drawn in August 1887, the figure on the left holds a train and a globe (which Voysey was obviously intending to replace with a ship). The figure on the right clutched a flash of lightning,

traditionally a symbol of war but here, probably, representing electricity. This symbolism was rather unclear and was therefore simplified in the final version, with a train on one side and a ship being transformed from wind to steam power on the other. In the central panel, too, the rather fussy arch was removed. But in this panel, it is the religious symbolism at its base that is most intriguing. Voysey held an ardent, if somewhat unorthodox, religious faith. His father had been a vicar, but was deprived of his living and expelled from the Church for denying the doctrine of everlasting hell. As his son put it, his father believed 'in a good God instead of an angry one'. Although C. F. A. Voysey, in his writings, constantly reiterates the need to respect the Creator and nature, he was antagonistic to religious dogma. Initially, the symbols of sacerdotalism in the central panel were intended 'to suggest the conflict between science and dogma'. After some months, the significance of these symbols was realized by the college authorities and, in October 1888, Seddon was ordered by the Building Committee to remove them.[43]

The triptych is a very early work; it was not until the 1890s that Voysey became established as a designer. Nevertheless, it shows some of the features that were to give Voysey's designs an international reputation. In a lecture that he gave in 1895 Voysey noted: 'Simplicity in decoration is one of the essential qualities without which no true richness is possible.' In revolt against the dull greens and sepias that predominated in fabric and wallpaper design at that time, he also declared: 'Let us do our utmost to raise the colour sense from morbid sickly despondency to bright and hopeful cheeriness, crudity if you will rather than mud and mourning.'[44]

The Aberystwyth mural is an early expression of Voysey's approach to design, as suggested by the above quotations. The three figures are stylized and flat. Simple forms predominate, so that Science's big toe becomes a simple oval. The linear forms filled with bold areas of colour stand out today as they did over a hundred years ago. Voysey's murals are not universally admired. Many find them puzzling. They have even been referred to as 'unfortunate'.[45] Indeed, in 1897, the college Building Committee decided to remove them.[46] Fortunately, the cost was prohibitive so the murals remain as an astonishingly bold proclamation of Seddon's belief in the unity of the visual arts and architecture.

The building contract stipulated that the science wing be completed by the beginning of the 1887–8 session. In the event there was a delay of six months, and the wing was not even partially ready for occupation until the beginning of the 1888 summer term. A major problem had arisen with the heating and ventilation system which Seddon entrusted to the Aeolus Company of Manchester. This company had developed a unique water-spray system, but at Aberystwyth this did not work. Tests carried out in July 1888 suggested that there was insufficient water pressure unless a cistern to hold 3,000 gallons was placed on the top of the great tower. There was a wrangle as to who should pay for this additional work and, when the system was needed in the autumn, it still did not function. The Building Committee now threatened to force the company to remove the apparatus. Matters were made even more difficult when the company became bankrupt. The trustee tried to get professional help to make the apparatus work, but to no avail. He was, however, able to come to an agreement with the college that the apparatus be left for college use on the payment of £50.[47] The affair considerably soured the relationship between Seddon and the Building Committee who patently began to doubt his understanding of recent technical developments. The heating and ventilation of the wing was put in the hands of a subcommittee who, in July 1889, gave a new contract to another Manchester firm, Haden and Company, who became responsible for heating the whole building and probably installed at the base of the main staircase the remarkable circular radiators that would delight a twentieth-century conceptual artist.

The Arts Wing

Work on the arts wing did not begin in earnest until the autumn of 1887. It was the hope that the whole building would be completed by the beginning of the 1888–9 session. The drawing-rooms that Seddon had situated on the seaward side of his hotel were now approached from the quadrangle that he had created in the northern wing, and were largely left intact, except for those that had to be reduced in size to accommodate the central staircase. The rooms on the ground and first floors were used as class-rooms and offices. The space on the second floor was kept in reserve for future use. There were more alterations on

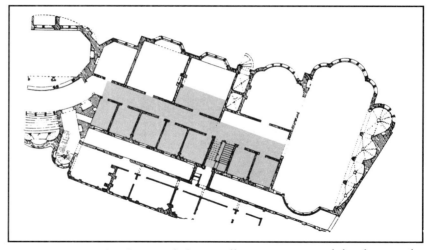

36. Plan of the north wing of the college, rebuilt as the arts wing, showing how the quadrangle was fitted into the original north wing.

37. The quadrangle.

the landward side. Some of the smaller rooms were joined to make class-rooms, while others were retained as rooms for individual members of staff. The varied windows, some extending over one floor and others two, that had been inherited from the hotel, were now used to light lofty class-rooms intermixed with smaller staff-rooms, some of

38. The roof of the
quadrangle showing the large
curved wooden beams
decorated with crests of the
Welsh counties.

which were located on a mezzanine floor above the ground floor. On
this mezzanine floor, too, there were windows looking into the
quadrangle that helped illuminate some of the rooms and staircases.
These windows were probably salvaged from the ruined building; in the
typical Seddon mode, they had columns as mullions. There were four
class-rooms on the ground floor with contiguous staff-rooms, and five
more class- and staff-rooms on the first floor. On the upper floors there
was much spare room. A gymnasium was situated on the fifth floor. The
students claimed that climbing the stairs was in itself 'not unworthy of a
place in the science of gymnastics'![48]

Considering the financial constraints to which Seddon was subjected,
the central staircase off the quadrangle was very grand. It is probable
that the marble pillars, its most opulent feature, were salvaged from the
hotel dining-room. A modicum of light was provided for the staircase by
two large circular apertures, each with eight cusps, opening into the
quadrangle. It was originally intended that the balcony would have iron
railings, but Seddon later decided to create a balustrade of moulded
concrete panels. True to his view that motifs from nature should only be

68

created in appropriate materials, Seddon confined himself, when decorating the panels, to a series of quatrefoils and cinquefoils. The balcony supports are also of concrete and are massive: they are a striking, if rather overwhelming, decorative feature. The quadrangle is lit from above. Large curved wooden beams support the roof, an extensive area of which consists of coloured glass panels: Seddon had 'medievalized' the roof of a London station such as King's Cross. The medieval effect was enhanced by the college decorating the ends of the beams with crests of the Welsh counties – to make manifest that the college served the whole of Wales. The quadrangle was to become the social hub of the college. As Dr Ellis recalls: 'The Quad (and its surrounding balcony) was the place to see and the place to be seen, and, over the years, it made every bit as important a contribution to the education of Aberystwyth students as any lecture-room or laboratory.'[49]

The large lecture and examinations hall at the north end of the quadrangle was entered through a double doorway. This is, today, the Old Hall. Except for the raking of the floor, its internal structure is unchanged from that of the great drawing-room that Seddon had designed in 1864. Although he no longer planned to have a vaulted ceiling, the aspidal projections at the west and east ends were retained, as was the vaulted aisle on the north side, with its arcade of marble columns and carved capitals. Much of the carving on the capitals and arches was abandoned when Savin became bankrupt, and remains today in its unfinished state.

In building the library, Seddon had a dilemma. Initially, as we have seen, he had intended lowering the whole arts wing to two storeys, and, as a result, to lower the height of the library also. Having later decided to retain the five storeys at the back of the wing, he found it difficult to match the library, which extended across the whole width of the building, with the higher rear portion. Furthermore, lowering the height of the library would destroy the upper storey of the great trefoil bay window that he had planned. He decided, therefore, to increase the overall height to that of the back part of the wing. This would provide space for two additional class-rooms over the rear part of the library, and would 'confer great dignity on the structure as seen from the Parade'.[50] It would also make possible the roof over the quadrangle.

The library comprised two connecting rooms. The larger room was 60 feet by 30 feet, and had added to it an impressive oriel on the western end that was raised some 21 inches 'so as to give additional dignity to the room and the charm of a view over the sea from the windows'.[51] There were two further recesses on the northern side of this room, one of which was in the tower on the north-western corner that Seddon never got a grant to complete. The room's most striking feature is the

39. A reconstruction of Seddon's original design for the library.

lofty and unusual trilobe barrel-vaulted ceiling, of a type that is found in some medieval churches in the Veneto such as San Zeno, Verona, and San Steffano, Venice.[52] In its original state this must have been even more impressive when the larger room was separated from the smaller by a high pointed arch. It was above this second room that the two additional class-rooms were situated.

Seddon's belief that raising the library roof would confer 'great dignity' on the building when seen from the north, was certainly borne out, even though he was not able to finish the tower at the north-west corner. Despite his financial difficulties, Seddon could not resist adding some decorative features, including a gargoyle of a demon! He also created a geometrical pattern on the north-west angle of the wing by varying the texture of the stone – the nearest he got to polychromy throughout the time he was involved with the building. He also added a frieze of miniature columns to the top of the trefoil library window, thus expressing the leitmotiv of the building in a new way. The rest of the front of the building remained intact after the fire, and was not altered. Included in the windows of the main rooms was coloured glass recovered from the windows of the former restaurant. Little change was made to the central block. The vaulting in the former bar area was not replaced, and, although the corbels remained, they no longer had a function. In rebuilding the great curved roof above the former billiard-room, Seddon removed the top lighting, giving it the clean-cut look of the new science wing.

The changes that Seddon made to his plans for the library inevitably meant an increase in cost, but, ever optimistic, he hoped that this could be met by other reductions and by using artificial instead of natural stone. His optimism proved unfounded and, in June 1888, he had to confess to the Building Committee that he now calculated that the estimate for the rebuilding would be exceeded. The committee were aghast to discover that Seddon had already spent an additional £665 on the library without authority.[53] The college was in a very difficult position. The Building Fund was exhausted, and already £6,000 had had to be borrowed from the bank.[54] The Council realized, however, that in view of the serious difficulties that would result from a 'rupture' with the architect and contractors at a time when the rebuilding was so far advanced, all that they could do was to accept the overspending and tell Seddon of 'their deep dissatisfaction that he should have permitted himself to so greatly depart from the clear and express terms of the contract'. For his part, all that Seddon could do was to express 'his regret for what had occurred, and his full assurance that it would not be repeated'.[55] The final accounts, drawn up in Febuary 1889, revealed that raising the library roof and the consequent alterations to the

70

chimneystacks and sea front had cost an additional £841. Improving the quadrangle had cost a further £275, and the rearrangement of the women students' rooms, and the provision of a separate women's entrance in King Street, sanctioned by the committee, had cost £388. In all, an additional cost of £1,800 had been incurred. The committee admitted, however, that the spending of this money had 'unquestionably added greatly to the utility and beauty of the building'. The total cost of the rebuilding, including furniture and fittings, was £24,816.[56]

Looking at the building today, we can see how remarkable the transformation achieved by Seddon was. We can thank him for being ruled by spirit and not by sense. However, at the time, this was not the view of many members of the college Council. Seddon's overspending, coupled with the Aeolus fiasco that dragged on into the autumn of 1889 and the delay in completing the building, effectively spelt the end of his connection with the college. When, in November 1889, W. T. Jones, a well-off Australian Welshman, offered to pay for the ornamental roof to cover the quadrangle, he stipulated that Seddon should not be employed to do the work – a proviso that surely must have been suggested to him by the principal or a member of the Council. It was decided, therefore, that Seddon's plans for the roof be purchased by the college for £25, and the work carried out by a local firm under the college's supervision. J. Ffoulkes Roberts was delighted. 'I understand', he wrote to the principal, 'that when we have paid for the plans we will be free of him for ever . . . We have managed to keep the dish even so far with Seddon and if possible let us do all in our power not to quarrel over the building – nevertheless I do not see how Seddon can be employed if we are to keep right with the donor and that must be done.'[57] In March 1890, the firm of Davies and Son, Newtown, was contracted to build the roof for £417.

5

The Completion of the College

In 1890, Principal T. C. Edwards toured the United States to appeal for money from Welsh expatriates to complete the college building. On the voyage out, he decided to focus on furnishing the new library. Edwards's mission was very successful; he returned with £876 and, ultimately, the Library Appeal Fund raised £1,050. In Febuary 1891, Edwards proposed to the college Building Committee that the library be fitted 'with shelves and cases etc., in accordance with designs from Mr C. J. Ferguson, Carlisle'.[1] It seems that Ferguson's name had been suggested to him by Stuart Rendel.[2] Early in May 1891, Edwards, after much deliberation, resigned to become principal of the Bala Theological College, and was replaced by T. F. Roberts. These changes resulted in a delay in implementing the library scheme. In the intervening period Seddon must have heard of the library proposals and, in October, he wrote to the college offering to revise the designs for the library fittings without charge, 'so that nothing be done out of harmony with the structure of the college'.[3] The Building Committee flatly refused to become involved with Seddon again. He was thanked for his 'kind offer', but as the work was not structural, and would not be out of keeping with the original design, the committee considered that 'it was not necessary to trouble him in the matter'.[4] Seddon, however, was not without his supporters. When the Building Committee minutes were presented to the college Council, there was strong opposition to the library plans. Some members believed, J. F. Roberts later noted, 'that Seddon would have done the work much better than Ferguson, so that an effort was made to get the work for Seddon'. It was only after much manœuvring that Roberts was able to get the Building Committee minutes adopted by the Council.[5]

Although Charles J. Ferguson (c. 1840–1904) practised from Carlisle, he also had a London office. He belonged to a younger generation than Seddon. In the 1860s, when Seddon was building the Castle House Hotel, Ferguson was articled to Sir Giles Gilbert Scott, Victorian Britain's most successful architect, who during his career was concerned with almost a thousand buildings of various types. The mainstay of Scott's practice was the building and restoration of churches, and he was a major apologist for High Victorian Gothic. Three major Gothic hotels were built in Victorian Britain: the Castle House Hotel, Aberystwyth, the Imperial Hotel, Great Malvern (1861–2), designed by E. W. Elmsie, and Scott's stunningly successful St Pancras Hotel (1869–72). In the 1860s and 1870s, however, there was a growing disenchantment amongst British architects with the Gothic revival. It was generally accepted that a refined form of Gothic was still the most suitable style for churches, but even here there was a preference for English rather than continental models and, within the English tradition, for Decorated or Perpendicular rather than Early English. Secular architecture was another matter. Disillusionment with the possibility of evolving a truly contemporary architecture based on Gothic resulted in a revival of interest in vernacular and Tudor buildings and, particularly, in the development of the 'Queen Anne' style: 'a flexible urban argot, sash windows, brick ribbed, based on late seventeenth century vernacular classicism, Dutch, French, Flemish, German and English – all seasoned with a dash of Japanese'.[6]

Mark Girouard has suggested that the Queen Anne style was developed by 'a circle that knew Burges and Seddon, but was a little apart from them'. He sees the 'remote origins' of the movement in Seddon's and Burges's membership of the Pre-Raphaelite and William Morris fraternity and in the furniture that they designed.[7] Norman Shaw, who became the leader of the movement, was certainly a member of the Rossetti–Morris circle.[8] Seddon, however, in common with most older Goths, abhorred Queen Anne architecture, and was particularly virulent in his attack on Norman Shaw.[9] But Shaw was supported by many young architects who now took the symbolic step of abandoning the pointed arch.[10] They included a group of young renegades working in Scott's office, many of whom, because of the rapid development of education in the years following the 1870 Elementary Education Act, became involved in designing schools and colleges. Thus J. J. Stevens (1831–1908) and E. R. Robson (1835–1917) were architects to the London School Board, and were responsible for replacing Gothic church schools with large Queen Anne elementary schools that symbolized the new secular age in education. G. F. Bodley (1827–1907), although best known for bringing about changes in church architecture, was responsible for the London School Board's grandiose offices on the Embankment built in a Franco-Dutch Queen Anne style. The new style was also adopted by T. G. Jackson (1835–1924) when designing the Oxford Examination Schools and the Oxford Boys' and Girls' Grammar Schools, and, perhaps most successfully of all, by Basil Champneys (1842–1935) in his design for Newnham College, Cambridge.

All these rebels from Scott's office were contemporaries of Ferguson, and he took their new approach to architecture to his Cumberland practice. Ferguson was an efficient and innovative architect. In 1865, while still articled to Scott, he won the competition for the design of Christ Church, Silloth, Cumberland. His design was, in Pevsner's estimation, 'quite ambitious': although Gothic in inspiration, with a broach spire and plate tracery, the interior was faced with yellow brick and red-brick trim, and with a band of brick used in projection and recession.[11] Another of Ferguson's churches, Bridlekirk (1868), had a neo-Norman doorway, but the interior was again brick-faced; this Pevsner thought both 'rather a shock' and 'daring'.[12] St Paul's, Pooley Bridge (1868), a small church, was designed by Ferguson in the Early English manner with lancet windows.[13] Gamblesey (1868) was in the style of the late thirteenth century, while the church of the Holy Ghost, Middleton, Westmorland (1878–9) was Perpendicular, and St Oswald, Burnside (1881–2) and St Aiden, Carlisle (1899–1902) were Decorated.[14] Ferguson's church architecture thus shows the stylistic eclecticism of the late-nineteenth-century church architect. Although his inspiration was always English, in each church a different style is dominant, with a gradual change from a preference for Early English to Decorated.

In his domestic architecture, Ferguson, typical of his generation,

40. The library after adaptation by Charles J. Ferguson.

74

looked to the Queen Anne movement for inspiration. In fitting the college library, he had a major problem. Seddon had created a lofty space, but little room for shelving. Ferguson thus built a balcony on two sides of the larger of the library spaces, but this crossed the central pointed arch. Ferguson filled the upper portion of the arch down to the level of the balcony, which was then supported by an arcade with two rounded arches – and this despite being adjacent to the double-pointed doorway that Seddon had created. Ferguson was proclaimimg his stylistic independence. The report of the opening ceremony of the library, which took place in November 1892, included an account that could well have been written by Ferguson. This attempted to justify the mixture of styles. 'In the best period of Gothic, the Decorated,' it notes, 'it was not at all unusual to use pointed and semi-circular arches together when the occasion required and with the best artistic results.'[15] The gallery has an iron framework, encased in the woodwork of the bookcases. Ferguson set the panelled returns of the bookcases to work in with the structural lines of the roof and recesses. The staircase to the gallery in the north-east corner of the room has two straight flights. The lower flight, the opening ceremony report notes rather portentously, 'as at St Cross, Winchester, projects somewhat into the room and forms a feature of it'. The style of the fittings is a vague Jacobean vernacular, with the balustrade echoing the round-headed arches below. As the report proclaims:

> The whole of the fittings have been executed in oak, following the national type of woodwork which was gradually developed in the sixteenth and following century when woodwork began to be used in forms suited to the material and free from the imitation of stonework of the earlier styles and culminated in that admirable British woodwork of the quiet domestic character which has not been excelled in any other country.

After their experience of Seddon, how delighted the Building Committee must have been to hear Ferguson suggest, when considering the lowest tender of £288 for the building work in the library, that perhaps plastering behind the bookcases was unnecessary and that the stonework could be done by a local man, so that the tender could be brought down to £190. He also suggested that a further reduction of £11 could be made by substituting brackets for the columns supporting the gallery, and that, furthermore, if the gallery was not made fireproof another reduction of £20 to £30 was possible. The committee had such confidence in Ferguson that, having accepted a tender of £696 for the shelving and fittings, they allowed him to go through the specifications and report to them any reductions that might be made 'without impairing the effect of the work'.[16] It is doubtful whether the college was in the least concerned about the discontinuity of styles that Ferguson

41. Alexandra Hall, the women's residence at the north end of the promenade, designed by C. J. Ferguson in Queen Anne style and built 1896–8.

brought about. He was well organized, he ensured that deadlines were respected and, most important of all, he kept within his budget. In any case, the stylistic variation in the library must have seemed very minor to those living through the Welsh chapel-building boom of the late nineteenth century.

In the 1890s there was a steady increase in the number of students in the college. In 1892, both a Day Training Department for elementary schoolteachers and an Agriculture Department were created, and these were housed in the unused space created by Seddon on the upper floors of the college building. During the 1880s the number of women students had increased markedly and a women's hall of residence became a priority. The Aberystwyth Corporation gave a site free of charge at the north end of the promenade, and the Pfeiffer Trust gave a grant of £2,000. With the hope of further contributions from friends of the college and a bank loan, the college decided in 1894 to build the women's hall, but with a strict upper spending limit of £15,000, including furniture. Rather than go to the expense of an architectural competition, it was decided to appoint Ferguson to design the hall, with T. E. Morgan, a local architect, to see to the day-to-day work.[17] In June 1896, the central and southern blocks were opened by Princess Alexandra, and two years later the north wing was added. Alexandra Hall, as designed by Ferguson, was in a cost-cutting Queen Anne style – with local stone, sash windows and Dutch gables.

The hall was far enough away from the college to prevent any clash of styles. Ferguson was presented with a much greater challenge when, in

76

1894, he was also invited to design a replacement for the Nash House and create a central block that would provide accommodation for the principal, registrar and the college administrators, as well as for the departments of agriculture, zoology and botany. All this was made possible by a Treasury grant of £10,000 with £5,000 collected from the public. Again there was a strict upper spending limit.[18] Before accepting the commission, Ferguson suggested that he should consult with Seddon, but the Building Committee did not think that this was necessary.[19] Nevertheless, Ferguson did contact Seddon, partly out of courtesy and partly to see if Seddon would loan him his plans. This Seddon did, but he also wrote to the college in high dudgeon. He recalled that when he last met the Council, on the completion of the reconstruction after the fire, the chairman had stated 'that it was with the regret of the Council that some fittings for the Library had been carried out under another architect from funds not under his control, but that it was the deliberate and express purpose of the Council that no work should be done to the structure itself during [his] lifetime except from [his] designs and under his superintendence'. Relying on the chairman's word, he had not charged for his design of the central block, the building of which was postponed because of the lack of funds. Seddon patently believed that the situation into which he had been placed in 1885 was being repeated, and that the Council, once again, was not free to offer the commission to another architect, and another architect was not free to accept it. Seddon, as in 1885, was happy to modify his design as required. No other architect, he again maintained, had his knowledge of the building, nor could 'do the work economically while preserving the general character of the building'. The Building Committee, however, was this time confident that Seddon had no claim on the college, and recommended that the appointment of Ferguson and Morgan be confirmed.[20] The college Council agreed, and Ferguson accepted the appointment.[21]

Seddon, now desperate, offered to work with Ferguson and Morgan. Otherwise, he demanded compensation for making the 1885 plans which, he estimated, amounted to £250. He had loaned his plans to Ferguson for the sake of the building and because Ferguson had 'behaved rightly'. But this did not prejudice any legal action he might take. The Council was unmoved; they informed Seddon that they had nothing to add to their earlier letter.[22] A year later, on 26 June 1896, the prince of Wales was to be installed as chancellor of the University of Wales at Aberystwyth, and Seddon wrote to the college asking if he could, as architect of the college building, be presented to the prince. He added, pathetically, that he had a chimneypiece 'with overmantle, executed in marbles, carved wood, and mosaic' which he had designed for the recess in the college library, which he valued at £500 and which he would present to the college, if the Council would consider his claim for compensation or refer the matter to the president of the RIBA. In such an event, he would also present the college with a large framed perspective drawing of the college as he had designed it. This could be hung in a temporary position during the prince's visit.[23] The Council again responded bluntly that they could see no reason to depart from their previous decision. Seddon, who must surely have now felt utterly snubbed, had no further communication with the college.

The architect's aim in designing the central block, the *Cambrian News* declared (in what might well have been Ferguson's words), was to create 'a bold rendering of free Gothic intended to form a centre to the bold and characteristic work of Mr Seddon'.[24] But, stylistically, the end-product had little in common with Seddon. Ferguson's instinct was nearer that of Nash who, before Price intervened, planned to make Castle House a 'square bit of architecture'. Ferguson had no understanding of Seddon's delight in sinuous curves; neither did he

share his abhorrence of right angles! At heart, Ferguson's four-storeyed central block is in the style of Board school Queen Anne. The most Seddon-like feature, the curved section on the town side, was included at the behest of the college Building Committee who requested 'that the outer walls on the King Street front be more curved so as to increase space and improve appearance'.[25] This curved section also made it possible for the 'sanitary tower' to be placed, not in the front of the block as first suggested, but in the rear, with the plumbing leading into an internal well.

The way in which Ferguson attempted to graft picturesque and vaguely Gothic features on to an un-Gothic façade is seen in the front of the block. Here, the *Cambrian News* reported, 'the windows are square-headed where light demands it: others are deeply-recessed arched heads, and others an outer area with a little attached tracery in the tympanums of the arches, with a great and imposing gable to the west of the south front.' All that Ferguson had achieved was to add different picturesque embellishments to sets of long lancet-type windows and, as a result, create stylistic chaos. At least he did not make the gables

Dutch! On the town side of the building, according to the *Cambrian News*, Ferguson had taken advantage of the irregular line of the frontage 'in the great bays and octagons which rise at different levels, and with the great roofs behind them give a varied and picturesque frontage to King Street'. In this area, it is the variety and the irregularity of the fenestration that is most startling – from the small windows in the 'sanitary tower' to the sets of five square-headed windows piled above each other from the first to the third floors and disguised to look Gothic with massive blind tracery in the tympanums and the areas between the floors. This is a type of intrusive decoration that Seddon would never have contemplated. More sympathetically, Ferguson added a storey to the block over the main entrance that linked the two sections of the building. This was executed in oak, and is set a little behind the parapets of the lower floors so as to be partially hidden. A stylistic link between the old and new buildings was created by Ferguson when he added parapets to Seddon's towers that were of the same design as those of the new block.

It is easy to be critical of the new central block. It is, however, as attractive as that proposed by Seddon in his 1885 design, and was certainly more utilitarian. Ferguson was far more aware than Seddon of the building's proposed use. One of his main concerns was fire prevention. The floors were 'on the Carlisle principle of fire-clay tubes and rolled steel joists'. The staircases were of steel and concrete, with bearers and handrails of wrought iron. The flats and gutters were of syssel asphalt on a foundation of concrete. The walls were of brick, faced with Greenshill stone, and the windows had internal lintels of steel and concrete. In this way it was hoped that the building was practically fireproof. Considerable attention was also given to the design of the laboratories and, particularly, to the extraction of fumes. Unlike Seddon, Ferguson had a reputation for the design of heating and plumbing systems, and was responsible for their installation in a number of great houses in the north of England, including Bamburgh Castle in Northumberland. The furnishing of the rooms was in yellow pine, except for those of the principal and registrar which were in oak. Included in the principal's room was a striking marble fireplace, the only remnant from Castle House. This, local tradition suggests, came from Hafod and is the work of Thomas Banks.

When the central block was opened on 26 October 1898, the Old College took on its present-day appearance. There have been a number of modifications over the years, but these have not altered the general look of the building. Fortunately, a scheme to add a storey to the science wing, designed by Ferguson, was abandoned in 1902 when it reached the tendering stage.[26] There was, however, in the same year, an internal

44. The marble chimneypiece in the principal's room; one of the few remnants from the original Castle House Hotel, it may be the work of Thomas Banks.

change of significance. Over many years the college had been presented with books and manuscripts of Welsh and Celtic interest by Sir John Williams, Principal T. C. Edwards and others, which it was hoped would be the nucleus of a national library of Wales. Following an appeal in 1897 for gifts and funds to purchase manuscripts and rare books, the collection had grown so large that it needed to be housed separately from the general library. It was decided, therefore, to enclose the bar area of the original hotel with a stone screen to create a separate room. This was designed by Ferguson.

In building the screen, it was necessary to remove Seddon's colonnade and, of course, the vista from the main entrance to the sea was blocked. Even so, a very handsome room was created. Ferguson included in the screen a number of windows of the sort that might be found in a small parish church. This ecclesiastical look was emphasized by the Building Committee when they chose glass with diamond panes for the windows.[27] As in the main library, Ferguson mixed the Decorated with rounded arches – this time for the double entrance doors that echoed the arches connecting the original building to the new central block. The separate, smaller library room again provides an instructive contrast between the approaches of Seddon and Ferguson to Gothic. Seddon's inspiration was Italian and French; that of Ferguson exclusively English. The fundamental premise of Seddon was that, with Gothic as the basic source, the architect should absorb a variety of styles which, in his case, included an extensive use of the classical column. In this way an individual style might be achieved. Ferguson's approach to eclecticism was to place features such as the rounded arch side by side with decoration from a specific period of English Gothic. To make a chemical analogy: Seddon was concerned in creating a unique compound; Ferguson a mixture. When the work of Seddon and that of Ferguson are juxtaposed, the result is a stylistic clash. This is nowhere more obvious than in this oval room created to house the Welsh library and, later, the science library.

In the 1890s, during the time that Ferguson was working in Aberystwyth, Seddon (who in 1886, on the death of Prichard, had been appointed architect to the Llandaff Diocese) was concerned mainly with renovating and building churches, church schools and vicarages. Much of his work in south Wales was, however, carried out by his partner, J. Coates Carter. Seddon was at this time increasingly active in London architectural life. In 1886 he was appointed editor of *Building World*. He became a prolific writer and was a member of a number of committees. He had had a long association with the Architectural Museum and, on the publication in 1902 of his catalogue of the museum's collection, *A Casket of Jewels*, he was presented with a silver bowl by the committee.

In the middle of these non-creative activities, Seddon continued to dream about designing a great and sublime building. At this time there was disquiet about Westminster Abbey being cluttered with monuments and, in 1890, a royal commission was set up to investigate. Seddon, in partnership with L. Harvey, submitted plans to the commission that proposed, amongst other features, a cluster of chapels around the chapter house and, at great cost, a huge Campo Santo that, if it had been built, would have dwarfed the abbey and the Houses of Parliament. Nothing came of this scheme, so Old College remained the nearest that Seddon got to designing a sublime structure. Little wonder that he was so distraught at not being allowed to complete his greatest building.

With the gradual movement of the college, in the 1960s and 1970s, to a new site overlooking Aberystwyth, the original college building became 'Old College' and a number of internal alterations were made. The examination hall floor was raked and the stage that had been constructed at the east end removed. This has exposed the 'segmented

45. Seddon's design of about 1890 for Monumental Halls in London. Nothing came of the scheme.

46. The Seddon Room, after conversion in 1976 from the science library into a committee room.

apse' and circular traceried windows that Seddon had included in his original Castle House Hotel design. Seddon's billiard-room was also transformed into a handsome council chamber but at the expense of many of its original features. When a new college library was opened in 1976, the former science library was refurbished as an elegant committee room and the college took the opportunity of paying tribute to Seddon by naming it the Seddon Room. It houses a portrait of Seddon, the perspective drawings he made of his designs for the Castle House Hotel and the college building, as well as some watercolours he painted of the Aberystwyth area. In April 1989, a commemorative plaque was erected to him. Ironically, it was placed on the outer wall of the central block designed by Ferguson.

It was J. Coates Carter who, in his obituary of Seddon in 1906, perhaps showed the greatest insight into his partner's achievement as an architect. He suggested that Seddon was 'by far the most original of the Gothic revivalists; for though among the strongest in his love for and belief in the revival, he was always a modern rather than a medievalist, even though he himself might not altogether have been willing to admit it; and in his work almost alone amongst the early revivalists was it impossible to trace the origin of the detail of any particular style or building.' Carter continues:

> In this respect he was certainly before his time. While others were content to produce copies more or less of ancient detail, he went deeper and sought to look behind the reasons that prompted medieval form, and to produce what a medieval designer would have done if living in the nineteenth century with the knowledge, historical and constructional, then available.

As late as 1970, Sir John Summerson, in his assessment of Seddon's Law Courts design, was stressing the appeal of his architecture to 'a modern age'. It is possible today to discern in Seddon's work a greater affinity with post-modernism. J. Mordaunt Crook has postulated that the dilemma of the architect in the late twentieth century is essentially that of the mid-Victorians: 'how to make use of an earlier language – with its disciplinary form and associative force – without succumbing to the dread disease of historicism.' As a result: 'Current wisdom suggests that the answer lies in "symbolic depth" rather than pastiche . . . an architecture of the future in a fusion of past and present.'[28] This is the time, therefore, to look at Old College with new eyes; the challenge that Seddon set himself is also ours.

Appendix: Recent Plans of Old College

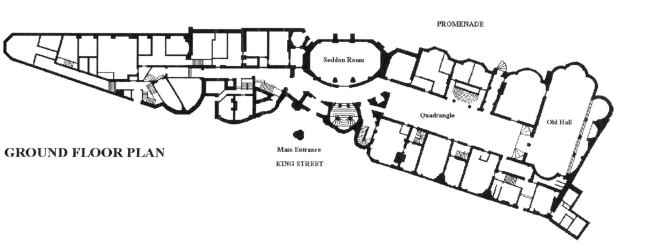

PROMENADE

Seddon Room

Quadrangle

Old Hall

GROUND FLOOR PLAN

Main Entrance
KING STREET

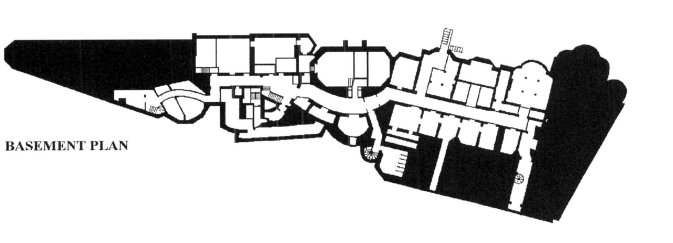

BASEMENT PLAN

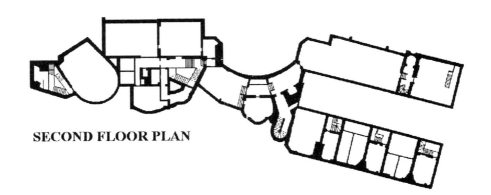

SECOND FLOOR PLAN

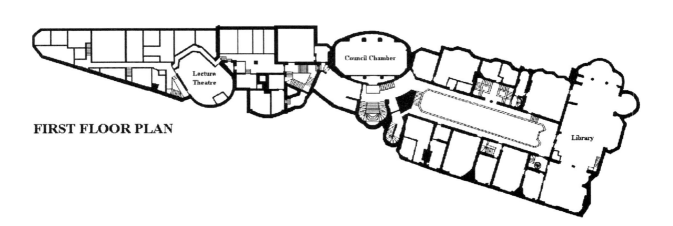

FIRST FLOOR PLAN

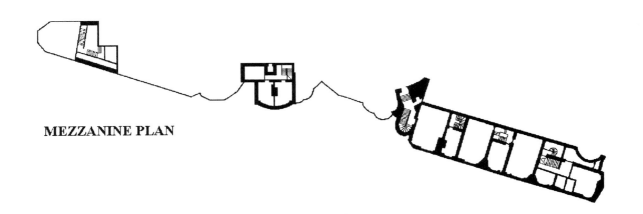

MEZZANINE PLAN

8th FLOOR

7th FLOOR

6th FLOOR

5th FLOOR

FOURTH FLOOR PLAN

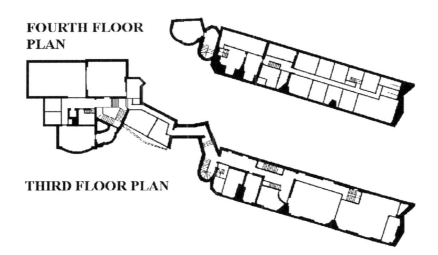

THIRD FLOOR PLAN

87

Notes

Notes to Chapter 1

1   Marcia Allentuck, 'Sir Uvedale Price and the Picturesque Garden: the
     evidence of the Colerton Papers', in Nikolaus Pevsner (ed.), *The Picturesque
     Garden and its Influence outside the British Isles* (Dumbarton Oaks, 1974),
     p. 59.
2   Uvedale Price, *An Essay on the Picturesque, as Compared with the Sublime and
     the Beautiful: And on the Use of Studying Pictures for the Purpose of Improving
     Real Landscape* (first edn., 1794; expanded edns. 1796–8, 1810). The
     quotations are from the 1810 edition.
3   For a full discussion of the movement see David Watkin, *The English Vision*
     (London, 1982).
4   E. Burke, *A Philosophical Enquiry into the Origin of our Ideas of the Sublime
     and Beautiful* (1757).
5   W. Gilpin, *Three Essays: On Picturesque Beauty; On Picturesque Travel; And on
     Sketching Landscape. To which is added a Poem on Landscape Painting* (1792).
6   Ann Bermingham, *Landscape and Ideology: The English Rustic Tradition,
     1740–1860* (London, 1987).
7   See Elisabeth Inglis-Jones, *Peacocks in Paradise* (London, 1950), Richard J.
     Moore-Colyer (ed.), *A Land of Pure Delight: Selections from the Letters of
     Thomas Johnes of Hafod* (Llandysul, 1992), and David Watkin, op. cit., pp.
     99–102.
8   Leslie Parris, *Landscape in Britain c. 1750–1850* (London, 1973), pp. 69–71.
9   Sir Uvedale Price to Sir George Beaumont, 18 March 1798, Colerton
     Papers, Pierpoint Morgan Library. Extensive extracts from this letter are
     reproduced in Marcia Allentuck, loc. cit., and in John Murdoch, 'A Villa in
     Arcadia', in Simon Pugh (ed.), *Reading Landscape: Country – City – Capital*
     (Manchester, 1990), p. 125.
10   Nikolaus Pevsner, *Studies in Art, Architecture and Design*, Vol. 1 (London,
     1968), p. 120. The reference is to Shelley's letters, 21 March 1821.
11   Sir Uvedale Price to Sir George Beaumont, loc. cit. All the quotations from
     Price that follow are from this letter.
12   W. J. Lewis, *Born on a Perilous Rock: Aberystwyth Past and Present*
     (Aberystwyth, 1980), p. 122.
13   Terence Davis, *John Nash, the Prince Regent's Architect* (London, 1973), pp.
     22–3.
14   Michael Mansbridge, *John Nash* (London, 1991), example 38.
15   For example, Nash in 1796–7 added a single-storey corner room, with

canopied balcony above, to the villa, Point Pleasant, that he was building at Kingston upon Thames, in order to provide sweeping views of the river. In 1799, he designed a very grand house, Sunridge Park at Bromley in Kent, whose ground-plan, in order to take advantage of a site overlooking the valley, followed closely that of Castle House (see Mansbridge, op. cit., examples 48 and 58).

16 Ann Bermingham, op. cit. p. 195.

17 W. J. Lewis, op. cit., p. 195.

18 *The Aberystwyth Guide* (1816), p. 26.

19 John Hilling, *Plans and Prospects: Architecture in Wales, 1780–1914*, catalogue of Welsh Arts Council Exhibition (1975), p. 44.

20 W. J. Lewis, op. cit., p. 171.

Notes to Chapter 2

1 For a summary of Seddon's career see Michael Darby, *John Pollard Seddon* (London, 1983), Introduction, pp. 11–14.

2 John P. Seddon, 'The Works of the PRB in Llandaff Cathedral', *Public Library Journal* (March 1903), p. 29.

3 Ibid.

4 Ibid.

5 J. P. Seddon, *Memoir and Letters of the Late Thomas Seddon, Artist* (1859), p. 9.

6 A. W. N. Pugin, *True Principles* (1841), p. 48 (quoted by J. Mordaunt Crook, *The Dilemma of Style: Architectural Ideas from the Picturesque to the Post-Modern* (London, 1987), p. 44.)

7 Stefan Muthesius, *The High Victorian Movement in Architecture, 1850–1870* (London, 1972), pp. 86–7.

8 J. P. Seddon, 'Spurious Eclecticism', *Building News*, 12 July 1872.

9 J. P. Seddon, 'The Modern European Style', *The Architect*, 14 March 1874.

10 G. P. Boyle, *Diaries*, 4 May 1858 (quoted by J. Mordaunt Crook, *William Burges and the High Victorian Dream* (London, 1981), p. 152).

11 There is a reproduction of *The Valley of Jehosephat* in the Tate Gallery catalogue, *The Pre-Raphaelites* (1984), p. 152.

12 J. M. Crook, *William Burges and the High Victorian Dream*, p. 75.

13 Seddon, however, was a more enthusiastic admirer of the Pre-Raphaelites than Burges, as their contributions to the debate at the twenty-first annual meeting of the Ecclesiological Society show (*The Ecclesiologist*, Vol. XVIII (1860), p. 249.

14 J. P. Seddon, *King René's Honeymoon Cabinet* (1898), p. 2.

15 This is J. M. Crook's phrase as in, for example, Crook, op. cit.(1987), p. 82.

16 J. M. Crook, op. cit.(1984), p. 50.

17 J. P. Seddon, *Progress in Art and Architecture* (London, 1852), p. 2.

18 John Ruskin, *The Seven Lamps of Architecture* (London, 1849). There is an assessment of Ruskin's influence on Seddon in Michael W. Brooks, *John Ruskin and Victorian Architecture* (London, 1989).

19 J. P. Seddon, op. cit. (1852), p. 12. This is a viewpoint that Seddon maintained throughout his career. In 1867, responding to a paper by Burges on 'Our Architectural Future', he decried his friend's pessimism and noted: 'There were many difficulties in the way of the student who desired to make

progress towards a new style of architecture, because it was the habit of people, when they saw designs of this sort, to shrug their shoulders and say it was not Gothic of the Middle Ages. He did not see why this should be, because the style of the thirteenth century was now obsolete, and he thought there ought to be something peculiar to the age in which we lived, so that artists might not be copyists, but inventors.' *The Builder*, 1 June 1867.

[20] Seddon, op. cit. (1852), p. 13.

[21] Ibid., p. 58.

[22] Ibid., p. 3.

[23] Ibid., p. 7.

[24] Ibid., p. 18.

[25] Ibid., pp. 30–1.

[26] Ibid., p. 39.

[27] Ibid., p. 41.

[28] *Public Library Journal* (March 1903), p. 29.

[29] Ibid.

[30] John B. Hilling, *Cardiff and the Valleys* (London, 1973), pp. 115–17.

[31] Seddon gives a full account of the works of the Pre-Raphaelites created for Llandaff Cathedral in a paper published in three parts in the *Public Library Journal* during 1903.

[32] Michael Darby, op. cit., p. 12.

[33] John Summerson, *Victorian Architecture: Four Studies in Evolution* (New York, 1970), p. 88.

[34] Ibid.

[35] Michael W. Brooks, op. cit., p. 120.

[36] Ibid.

[37] John Summerson, op. cit., p. 88.

[38] Charles L. Eastlake, *A History of the Gothic Revival*, ed. J. Mordaunt Crook (Leicester, 1970), pp. 304–6.

[39] Mark Girouard, *The Victorian Country House* (Oxford, 1971), p. 36.

[40] Geoffrey Tyack, 'A Victorian Architectural Correspondence', *Architectural History*, Vol. 22 (1979), p. 79.

[41] Seddon to Shirley, 24 Dec. 1862, quoted by Tyack, ibid.

[42] Prichard to Shirley, 18 March 1863, quoted by Tyack, ibid.

[43] J. P. Seddon, op. cit. (1898), Preface.

[44] For example, the Boyce diary for 19 July notes: 'Rossetti and Swinburne called to see me. We went down to Burges's room. After tea, Burges, Seddon and Rossetti went off to "Judge and Jury". Swinburne and I get some ices.' J. M. Crook, op. cit. (1981), p. 307.

[45] W. M. Rossetti, *Some Reminiscences* (London, 1906), p. 144 (quoted in Michael Darby, op. cit., p. 14).

[46] J. M. Crook, op. cit. (1981), p. 307.

[47] Michael Darby, op.cit., p. 14.

[48] Clive Wainwright, 'Pre-Raphaelite Furniture', in J. Mordaunt Crook (ed.), *The Strange Genius of William Burges: Art and Architecture, 1827–1881* (Cardiff, 1981), p. 69.

[49] *Building News*, 1 May 1863, p. 329.

1   W. J. Lewis, op. cit., p. 200.

2   From a speech by Savin at a dinner held at the Belle Vue Hotel on 22 July
    1864 to mark the formal opening of the railway (*Aberystwyth Observer*, 30
    July 1864).

3   Ivor Thomas, *Top Sawyer* (Golden Grove Edition, 1988), pp. 56–61.

4   J. P. Seddon, 'On the University College of Wales and Other Buildings at
    and near Aberystwyth', *Trans. Royal Inst. of British Architects* (1871–2), pp.
    148–52. Unless stated otherwise, all the quotations by Seddon relating to
    the Castle House Hotel are from this paper.

5   *Aberystwyth Observer*, 6 August 1864.

6   *Building News*, 28 Dec. 1866.

7   J. M. Crook (ed.), *A History of the Gothic Revival* by Charles L. Eastlake
    (1872; new edn. Leicester,1970), p. 305.

8   Ransome's Patent Stone was manufactured at Ipswich and was made by
    mixing stone with chemicals so that it could be easily moulded. Seddon was
    so attracted to this material that he proposed using it for an elaborate
    fountain to be sited in Australia (Michael Darby, op. cit., p. 104).

9   *Aberystwyth Observer*, 16 Dec. 1865.

10 Nikolaus Pevsner, *A History of Building Types* (London, 1976), p. 178.

11 Roger Dixon and Stefan Muthesius, *Victorian Architecture* (London, 1978),
    p. 79.

12 Ibid., p. 80.

13 There is some confusion about the origin of the stone used for the outer
    walling. In his 1871 paper to the RIBA, Seddon refers to the Cefn Quarry
    owned by Savin. Iwan Morgan (ed.), *The College by the Sea* (Aberystwyth,
    1928), p. 37, refers to the stone as 'Cefn-Greensill'. The *Building News* (28
    Dec. 1866) refers to the Cefn Quarry but locates it in Cheshire. The
    Greenshill Quarry in Shropshire was easily accessible by rail, and Greenshill
    stone was used for the windows and other decorations of stations on the
    Cambrian Line. (See, for example, the station building at Welshpool which is
    now alongside the Welshpool bypass.) Greenshill stone was certainly used by
    Seddon and Ferguson in their later reconstruction of the college. (I am
    indebted to Mr Peter Hendry for finding information on the source of the
    stone.)

14 J. Coates Carter, 'John Pollard Seddon', *RIBA Journal*, 13 (1905–6), p. 221.

15 These windows are so deeply set that an American architectural historian,
    who was presumably working from a photograph, thought that they were
    doors (George L. Hersey, *High Victorian Gothic* (Baltimore, 1972), p. 152).

16 In the National Library of Wales, Aberystwyth, is deposited probably the
    only plan of the northern section of the hotel. This is too damaged to
    reproduce, but it shows that bedrooms were to be built over the drawing-
    room.

17 H. S. Goodhart-Rendel, *English Architecture since the Regency* (London,
    1953), p. 106.

18 The head of the woman in the Welsh hat might have been added later,
    perhaps after the fire of 1885.

19 Iwan Morgan (ed.), op. cit., p. 32. Morgan's account of the building of the
    Castle House Hotel contains interesting details not found elsewhere.
    Unfortunately, he does not cite his sources.

20 Ibid.
21 *Building News*, 24 Nov. 1865.
22 *Aberystwyth Observer*, 18 Aug. 1866 (supplement).
23 John Summerson, op. cit., p. 111.
24 *Building News*, 28 Dec. 1866.
25 Dixon and Muthesius, op. cit., p. 81.
26 H-R. Hitchcock, *Architecture: Nineteenth and Twentieth Centuries* (Harmondsworth, 1977), p. 265.

Notes to Chapter 4

1   E. L. Ellis, *The University College of Wales, Aberystwyth 1872–1972* (Cardiff, 1972), p. 27.
2   J. P. Seddon, 'On the University College of Wales', op. cit. (1871–2), p. 150.
3   *The Architect*, 2 July 1870.
4   E. L. Ellis, op. cit., p. 29.
5   Ibid., p. 42.
6   Ibid., p. 46.
7   Ibid., p. 42.
8   Iwan Morgan (ed.), op. cit., p. 38.
9   J. E. Lloyd, 'A Retrospect 1877–1881', in Iwan Morgan (ed.), op. cit., p. 71.
10 Minutes of Governors of the University College of Wales (UCW), 20 Jan. 1875.
11 Minutes of UCW Council, 9 Oct. 1877 and 12 March 1878.
12 For a general account of the Report see W. G. Evans, 'The Aberdare Report and Education in Wales', *Welsh History Review*, 11 No. 2 (Dec. 1982), pp. 150–73. The Report's implications for the college are discussed in Ellis, op. cit., ch. 3, 'The Ishmael of Colleges'.
13 Minutes of UCW Council, 21 Oct. 1884.
14 Malcolm Seaborne, *Schools in Wales, 1500–1900: A Social and Architectural History* (Denbigh, 1992), p. 179.
15 J. F. Roberts to T. C. Edwards, 2 Dec. 1884 (T. I. Ellis (ed.), *T. C. Edwards Letters* (Aberystwyth, 1952), letter 402, p. 232).
16 *The Builder*, 27 Dec. 1884.
17 Seddon to President of the Council, 19 Jan. 1885 (Minutes of UCW Council, 20 Jan. 1885).
18 Minutes of UCW Council, 20 Jan. 1885.
19 Ibid., 18 March 1885.
20 A vivid account of the college fire is given by J. Brough, 'The Fire of 9 July 1885', in Iwan Morgan, op. cit., pp. 47–52.
21 E. L. Ellis, op. cit., p. 87.
22 J. Viriamu Jones to T. C. Edwards, 14 July 1885 (T. I. Ellis, op. cit., item 431, p. 247).
23 H. B. Jones to J. B. Rogers, 18 Sept. 1885, quoted by E. L. Ellis, op. cit., p. 88.
24 Mary Edwards to T. C. Edwards (telegram), 9 July 1885 (T. I. Ellis, item 425, p. 245).
25 Minutes of UCW Council, 14 July 1885.
26 Minutes of UCW Building Committee, 30 July 1885.
27 Ibid., 29 Aug. 1885.

28 E. L. Ellis, op. cit., p. 89.
29 *The Builder*, 7 Nov. 1885.
30 Memorial signed by 115 of the 128 students, Oct. 1885. Reproduced in Iwan Morgan, op. cit., p. 95.
31 Minutes of UCW Council, 31 May 1885.
32 Minutes of UCW Building Committee, 29 July 1886.
33 Ibid.
34 Ibid., 19 Oct. 1886.
35 Ibid.
36 'The New College', *UCW Magazine*, Vol. IX, No. 3, Feb. 1887, pp. 97–104.
37 J. P. Seddon to Building Committee, 18 Oct. 1886 (Minutes of UCW Building Committee, 19 Oct. 1886).
38 Ibid., 22 Feb. 1887.
39 J. F. Roberts to T. C. Edwards, 23 Aug. 1886 (T. I. Ellis, op. cit., item 545, p. 259).
40 J. Coates Carter, 'John Pollard Seddon', *RIBA Journal*, 13 (1905–6), p. 221.
41 Minutes of UCW Building Committee, 6 Dec. 1888.
42 John Brandon Jones *et al.*, *C. F. A. Voysey: Architect and Designer, 1857–1941* (Brighton, 1978), p. 17.
43 Voysey wrote about the central panel: 'a bearded figure denoting science is sitting on a throne, the base of which bore the symbols of sacerdotalism. The meaning briefly stated was, to suggest the conflict between science and dogma. The panel remained in position for many years until one day high authority awakened to its meaning and as reported the objectional parts were removed. The so called "objectional parts" be it noted were the symbols of sacerdotalism' (John Brandon Jones, ibid., p. 37). As the minutes of the college Building Committee show, the 'objectional parts' were removed after a few months rather than years.
44 'The Aims and Conditions of the Modern Decorator', lecture by C. F. A. Voysey, *Journal of Decorative Art*, XV (15 Feb. 1895), p. 82, quoted by Elizabeth Aslin, in 'Pattern Design', in Brandon Jones, ibid., p. 96.
45 Iwan Morgan, op. cit., p. 42.
46 Minutes of UCW Building Committee, 19 Oct. 1897.
47 Ibid., 1 July 1889.
48 Iwan Morgan, op. cit., p. 43.
49 E. L. Ellis, op. cit., p. 104.
50 Minutes of UCW Building Committee, 7 June 1888.
51 Report of Library opening ceremony, Iwan Morgan, op. cit., p. 206.
52 I am indebted to Mr Phil Thomas for this point.
53 Minutes of UCW Building Committee, 7 June 1888.
54 Minutes of UCW Council, 8 June 1888.
55 Ibid., 17 July 1888.
56 Ibid., 1 May 1889.
57 J. F. Roberts to T. C. Edwards, 8 Jan. 1890 (T. I. Ellis, op. cit., item 494, p. 281).

Notes to Chapter 5

1 Minutes of UCW Building Committee, 7 Feb. 1891.
2 J. F. Roberts to T. C. Edwards, 15 Oct. 1891 (T. I. Ellis, op. cit., item 514, p. 293).

3 Minutes of UCW Building Committee, 12 Oct. 1892.

4 Ibid.

5 J. F. Roberts to T. C. Edwards, 15 Oct. 1891.

6 J. Mordaunt Crook, op. cit. (1987), p. 170.

7 Mark Girouard, *Sweetness and Light: The 'Queen Anne' Movement, 1869–1900* (Oxford, 1977), p. 13.

8 Ibid., p. 25.

9 In a letter to the *Building News* (1880), p. 237, Seddon noted 'If style be rhythm, commonsense and appropriateness, . . . there is no such thing as a style belonging to Queen Anne; but merely stuffing a few parodied false features of Classic upon all that was left, but fast dying out, of the true, homely and comfortable structures left us from the Middle Ages.' In a later letter (p. 297) he wrote: 'no man knows better than Mr Norman Shaw . . . that his practice is indefensible, except that it may be making his fortune: and much good, under the circumstances, is it likely to do him. Architectural features are a recognised language, and to make a hash of them is treason to the profession.'

10 J. Mordaunt Crook, op. cit. (1987), p. 206.

11 Nikolaus Pevsner, *Cumberland and Westmorland* (Harmondsworth, 1967), p. 189.

12 Ibid., pp. 77–8.

13 Ibid., p. 284.

14 Ibid., pp. 126, 276, 263 and 296.

15 Quoted in Iwan Morgan, op. cit., p. 206.

16 Minutes of UCW Building Committee, 2 March 1892.

17 Ibid., 7 Feb. 1894.

18 E. L. Ellis, op. cit., p. 177.

19 Minutes of UCW Building Committee, 15 May 1895.

20 Minutes of Special Building Committee, 21 May 1895.

21 Minutes of UCW Council, 22 May 1895.

22 Ibid., 28 June 1895.

23 Ibid., 30 Sept. 1896.

24 *Cambrian News*, 28 Oct. 1898.

25 Minutes of Building Subcommittee, 12 Sept. 1892.

26 Minutes of UCW Building Committee, 17 June 1902.

27 Ibid., 21 Nov. 1902. It was estimated that the screen would cost £275 and the shelving £181.

28 J. Mordaunt Crook, op. cit. (1987), pp. 267–8.

Bibliographical Note

In my attempt to understand the tortuous development of Victorian architecture, I derived the greatest help from the pioneering researches of Professor J. Mordaunt Crook: his new edition (Leicester, 1970) of Charles L. Eastlake's *A History of the Gothic Revival* (first published in 1872); his study of the life and work of William Burges, *William Burges and the High Victorian Dream* (London, 1981); his magisterial survey *The Dilemma of Style: Architectural Ideas from the Picturesque to the Post-Modern* (London, 1987). Essential reading, too, are Stefan Muthesius's seminal *The High Victorian Movement in Architecture, 1859–1870* (London, 1972) and Roger Dixon and Stefan Muthesius, *Victorian Architecture* (London, 1978). Henry-Russell Hitchcock, *Architecture: Nineteenth and Twentieth Centuries* (Harmondsworth, 1977) places British developments in their European context. The development of architecture in Wales is surveyed by John B. Hilling in *Cardiff and the Valleys* (Cardiff, 1973) and *The Historic Architecture of Wales* (London, 1975).

Michael Darby, *John Pollard Seddon* (London, 1983), not only contains an invaluable catalogue of almost two thousand designs by Seddon deposited at the Victoria and Albert Museum, but also a chronology of the buildings that Seddon designed, his publications and other professional activities, as well as a brief account of his life. The only study that gives serious attention to Seddon's *Progress in Art and Architecture* is Michael W. Brooks, *John Ruskin and Victorian Architecture* (London, 1989) – a book that also throws considerable light on the High Victorian movement as a whole. Researchers concerned with the history of the University at Aberystwyth, or of the town, are fortunate to have available to them E. L. Ellis, *The University College of Wales, Aberystwyth, 1872–1972* (Cardiff, 1972) and W. J. Lewis, *Born on a Perilous Rock: Aberystwyth Past and Present* (Aberystwyth, 1980). I have made much use of both books.

Index